SURVIVING RELATIONSHIPS

ALEXANDRA LEE PAIGE

Copyright © 2019 Alexandra Lee Paige.

All rights reserved. No part of this book may be reproduced, stored, or transmitted by any means—whether auditory, graphic, mechanical, or electronic—without written permission of the author, except in the case of brief excerpts used in critical articles and reviews. Unauthorized reproduction of any part of this work is illegal and is punishable by law.

ISBN: 978-1-950147-00-7 (sc)
ISBN: 978-1-950147-01-4 (e)

Publishing Information:
Paige Publishing
10120 Main St.
Clarence NY 14031
254-371-7941

Because of the dynamic nature of the Internet, any web addresses or links contained in this book may have changed since publication and may no longer be valid. The views expressed in this work are solely those of the author and do not necessarily reflect the views of the publisher, and the publisher hereby disclaims any responsibility for them.

First Edition
Cover Design and Formatting by Cassy Roop of Pink Ink Designs

Lulu Publishing Services rev. date: 11/22/2019

Surviving
RELATIONSHIPS

Dedication

I would like to dedicate this book to my sons for the love and support they provided during these demanding relationships. If it weren't for you two going along with me on this journey, I might have lowered my expectations of what type of love I was searching for and may have managed to lose myself during the process. I would like to show appreciation to my mother, for giving me an example of what a strong-willed individual can accomplish if he or she continues to possess a positive worldview on life. To my brothers, we all have endured many things through the years and I would like to thank you both for always being an anchor. To my soulmate, you are truly a godsend and I couldn't be more thankful for your love, kindness, and understanding heart. I look forward to many more years of adventures by your side.

Table of Contents

Chapter One: The Foundation.............1
Chapter Two: The Lessons Learned.............7
Chapter Three: Avoidable.............15
Chapter Four: The Antics.............21
Chapter Five: Improvised.............31
Chapter Six: The Spontaneity.............37
Chapter Seven: The Contamination.............45
Chapter Eight: Nonsensical.............55
Chapter Nine: The Cheating.............65
Chapter Ten: The Physical Abuse.............73
Chapter Eleven: The Sexual Abuse.............81
Chapter Twelve: This Is My Beginning.............89
Word from the Author.............95
Eight Rules of Thumb.............99

Introduction

I have been told by numerous people throughout my life that I should write a book because my story could potentially help others out of certain situations. I told my husband that I was waiting for the right time to write my book, he flat out told me that I was being selfish because I could possibly save someone's life who had the opportunity to read my story. By putting my book on hold, I was depriving someone of being reached by my information. I decided right then and there to stop shuffling my feet with the intent of opening my life for the world to view, judge, and comment on. I have managed to acquire a certain character of knowledge through first-hand experience with relationships. I'm hoping to reach anyone who has or is currently involved in a relationship that he or she may be questioning whether to stay and fight or walk away. I don't want to bore you with a big set up, so here's my story.

I managed to beat the odds of becoming a teen mother at the mere age of 16 and completed high school at the age of 17. I moved out on my own and began my journey in life the day I turned 18. Often working two jobs at a time, I made it my goal in life to always be independent and raise my children with the best of everything that I could possibly provide. The only thing missing from my world would be the completion of what America used to call a cookie-cutter family. You know the one, typical mother and father, two kids, a car, a house, and the white picket fence. Little did I know, that was not in the plans for me and I wouldn't even experience my version of real love for the first time until my late 30s.

You name it, I've been through it all and much more than I expected, all at the hands of individuals who I thought would improve my situation. Not the case at all, it turns out that the best times my children and I shared, was when I was single and there wasn't a man in sight. I quickly learned that we shape our future by the partners we choose and exactly how much of someone else's behavior we're willing to live with. As naïve as I was starting out in this big bright world, I managed to get hit with a few hard lessons which made me toughen up sooner than I had imagined.

I have always been someone who enjoys my alone time, but when I was sharing my time and space with another, this is when I would go in open-minded and wait to see what would happen with this new experience. It always starts out the same, we're nice to one another, get on each other's nerves, and then things would just turn super frivolous. For some reason I'm always surprised that someone would hurt me, cheat on me, and even have the nerve to turn violent against me. Why? What is it about me that told these individuals they could practically get away with causing me much pain?

Those were my younger years, still wet behind the ears and unfamiliar with the dissimilar personalities that came my way. I began to turn into someone who no longer gave respect to another person who didn't deliver it to me. I started to demand respect and began to hate the world because my perception shifted the more I got used by the people I trusted. I stopped fighting for what I thought a relationship should be, because I wasn't getting anyone who fit the mold. Entering in my early 30s I was depleted; I was finished with the fight and started to accept the fact that I had to make my own happiness because the grocery store wasn't mixing up a batch of it and selling it by the pound. I began to put myself out there and tell other interested parties who I was without a care in the world. If they liked me, we could go from there, and if they didn't, they could move on. Lo and behold, after all the failed attempts at trying to force individuals into the idea of "family" that I had in my head, it was when I *wasn't* looking, he appeared.

There is life after the hardships you've endured at the beginning of your travels through life that you will eventually overcome. I am a living testament to that statement. Life will take us on many adventures and we *will* embark on some tough times, times that will make us question the purpose of certain experiences. It is a must that we learn to challenge ourselves when we are irresolute and muster up the nerve to be assertive when we feel like someone is purposely taking advantage of our kindness and our heart. When I met my soulmate, I never had to worry about either of those things. He worried about them for me, even to the point where he took the initiative to eliminate the people he saw being mischievous from my life. I have never had a protector like him who not only looked out for my best interest, but also took the necessary steps to help me see what types of people I have allowed in my circle. It is a blessing to have someone by your side who not only fights for your affection but fights for your sanity when you continue to put yourself in harm's way by entertaining other people's shenanigans.

I am no longer that fresh-faced young girl who entered the world with wide eyed expectations and a pure heart. In order for me to understand the world, I had to experience some of the darkest of its crevices when dealing with the individuals who make up our humankind. As strange as all of this may sound, I wouldn't change any encounter that I went through because it's what shaped me into the person I am today. After reading this book, some of you might take that last sentence and say that I am crazy for not wanting to change any of the ordeals, affairs, violent episodes, or even the lost life I had to live without. My answer to that is, I would not have the wisdom and understanding of how people are if I didn't go through it firsthand. Also, these things have made me appreciate the man that I currently share my life with more than I ever would if I did not engage with individuals from my past who were confrontational, bloodthirsty, and narcissistic.

I've learned to acknowledge when I am wrong in a situation, to be grateful when my life is blessed with people who hold a high value of substance, and to enhance those around me who can genuinely implement the knowledge I've acquired over time, to flourish their perception in a positive manner. I tell people all the time, I'm the nicest person you'll ever meet, just don't get on my bad side. Those words are true and I'm happy to say that my bad side hasn't been tested for many years. We grow and learn from our past endeavors, and if they hit home, we take that information and apply it to our life so that we can guide our children to a better existence.

Speaking of which, I give ample amounts of advice in this book and most of it is about relationships with your significant others, but a lot of it involves the bonds you share with your children. Some of the mistakes I made in my life, my children were able to see and vocalize their opinion one way or another. While I didn't always take their advice because I felt I could handle the situation, I was lucky to have them as allies. They looked out for me and I appreciate that because children tend to live their life based on how they view their parent/s' firsthand experiences. I regret some of the things my children have heard or seen because of my choice to continue a relationship that I knew was over as soon as the disrespect entered our home. In retrospect, I should have walked away from any situation that caused me harm, unhappiness, and hurtful tears. Your children are innocent, and they don't see the bad unless it's presented to them on a platter. Please take your actions into consideration when you have children who may end up walking in your footsteps because this is the only example of "disguised" love that you opted to show them!

We all have an option of choosing to stay in a disturbed relationship while we grin and bear it to the end. I know now that I never have to put up with someone else's incompetence because they don't know how to love me in the proper manner. We don't have to live with someone shoving insulting words down our throat when they we are incapable of knowing who we are as a person. These types of individuals thrive on taking advantage of someone's feelings for their own merriment. Choose to walk away and leave that person behind so you can make yourself available for a companion who will better suit the needs of who you want to share the years of your life. When you can look at your significant other and say, I hope my child ends up with someone like you, you've made an appropriate choice and that person is most likely a good role model for your child to emulate.

Walk with me if you will, into my journey of relationships and take notice of the change in my demeanor as my life experience alters my worldview. While I am happy to present my life in its rawest state possible with the intent of helping others get out of a harmful situation, I am fearful of the world knowing my truth. I will no longer protect those from my past because someone else's future depends on *this* attestation. I wish to bring hope to those who have lost themselves in a significant other's mental or physical abusive behavior. I want to encourage anyone reading this book to aspire to recognize their self-worth, gain confidence in their ability to walk away, and achieve a healthier life with the possibility of welcoming love in the future.

Chapter One

THE FOUNDATION

AS CHILDREN, WE EMULATE those who are in our home when we began to develop behavioral patterns. I am no different when it comes to this notion. One of the first relationships I saw growing up was difficult to witness. For someone on the outside looking in, our family (at the time) looked much like any other. My mother endured more than she had to when it came to her ex-husband, behind closed doors and after a few drinks, the scene changed significantly. I could tell what type of day it was going to be when I came home from school immediately after I got inside and closed the door.

If he hadn't been drinking that day, everything was normal, and I could relax without worry, everyone was safe. On the other hand, if old-school music was playing, he had glazed over eyes, and liquor on his breath, a weary feeling would consume me, and I'd just wait to see how it all played out. My best defense was to stay out of his way, not be seen, or go to a friend's house. When my mother came home, it was either going to be a calm night or a horrible scene from the Tina Turner movie, What's Love Got to Do with It. Hearing and sometimes seeing the abuse stowed upon my mother was eye-opening for me because this is the first vision of love that I had when it came to a reference of a real marriage. I say real because when I would watch TV shows and movies, they never played out to what was my reality.

I often wondered why my mother didn't kicked him out for good; why was it so easy (in my young eyes) for her to allow him to keep coming back after the nights in jail? Why didn't she divorce him after the very first time he hurt her physically? Surely someone at her place of business saw what she was hiding behind the makeup and would step in to save her. Why would the neighbors be the one to call the police, but would avoid eye contact when they saw us coming or going (like we were the monsters)? How could it be, that so many outsiders knew what was going on in our home behind closed doors, but refuse to act? Why wasn't life so easy that she could just pack us up and walk away from this hazardous situation? Why was it our responsibility to keep the secret of someone else's damaging behavior when we were the ones who were getting tormented by his negative actions? I had so many questions that no one could give me the answers to that would make sense.

Ultimately, my mother got tired of fighting for her life. I mean that in the most literal way possible with the intent of driving it home. Please understand that I never once in all my days on earth viewed my mother as weak. She's the strongest person I know and even with everything that this man put her through, she was always victorious! I personally think that's something that he recognized within her and decided within himself that he was going to try his best, to beat it out of her. She always made sure we had the best of any and everything that we wanted. Going through that divorce meant challenging times for us all, but she always made the best out of our life until we got past it. She sheltered us from the stress of the divorce by always putting on a good forcover face. When the storm was over, we knew it because there was an aura about her personality that returned. She began to mentally and physically work on herself which restored the damage. Where once she was covered with clothes from head to toe hiding every inch of her bruised body, she now was a bodybuilder winning trophies and strutting her stuff across the stage.

When my mother decided to be a single parent, I'm sure there were many things that crossed her mind which didn't work in her favor.

Nevertheless, she stuck to her guns and got out of the situation with the intent of providing a better life for me and my siblings. Once we were on our own, life seemed peaceful, fearless, and exciting through my eyes. She worked a lot, but she always made time to take us on trips, expand our horizons by introducing us to things we never tried before, and teaching us the value of family bonding. She made sure to instill in us that she will not always be here, so we had to learn to depend on each other because we are all we have in this world. I no longer felt the need to spend the night at someone else's house, because she made our home a safe haven. This is not to say that she wasn't hard on us, she always meant business because she pushed us to *want* to do better in our lives. Therefore, it was crucial for me to always grow from every relationship I had, knowing that I can always improve my situation because no matter what, I have the option to walk away.

LOOKING BACK

I DIDN'T KNOW it at the time, but her relationship with that individual, ultimately set the tone for what was to come in my future interactive relations. It's funny how we look back on certain situations and see how they affect us as adults. Some things we block out and some things we cherish, but overall, we can take these lessons and use them to our advantage as we move forward. I learned from my mother's relationship with this individual that just because someone disguises themselves as love doesn't mean that they truly love you from the heart. Your heart is your life, so why let others play with it who don't care if you live or die broken or strong. My mother chose to live healthy and strong without that black cloud of fear hanging over her head on a daily basis. Instead of constantly walking around broken just to make it through the day, she chose to eliminate the malevolent individual who obtained his power from being malicious.

Those who build you up and support you through life are truly keepers because they are not playing against you, they simply want to see you succeed so you both can achieve personal growth by being in each other's lives. My mother always knows how to turn a negative into a positive by sheltering us and focusing on surviving. Either way, we always seem to end up on top no matter what outsiders try to do to us. We usually take time to reevaluate what just happened, and then we bounce back with a vengeance by sheltering (protecting against) and surviving (returning to fight again).

The example that my mother set for me over the years is that, you are what you tolerate. When you get tired of dealing with someone else's chaos, you wake up and realize that you've had enough. That's when you know you're ready to walk away, note that being ready to walk away is not the same as doing so. When you're ready to walk away, that's when you start to build up strength within yourself to follow through. You get all your ducks in a row (so to speak), and once you build up enough courage, stability, and backbone to walk out the door, you make your move. When you have swallowed more than your share of deceitfulness, infidelity, and contradicted behavior that whatever that person has to say to get you to stay, won't matter anymore because you've heard it all before and you know you'll be at this very exact point two months from now when another epiphany hits you in the face.

Don't allow an individual to keep pulling you back into a situation that you know is unrealistic for you to live in without damaging your character. You know this person is toxic and the only way for you to walk out of this situation unscathed is for *you* to discover that you deserve better. I know at times it's hard to fathom, but there is someone out there going through similar situations and relationships as you are, that will be ready when you're ready to take on the world with you. This is something that I had to convince myself of over time because I wasn't ready to accept that I deserved a man who was kindhearted, giving, loving, and respectful. I didn't know how to love because I didn't love myself enough to show true love to another individual. The only real love that I witnessed was the love my mother had for her children, so I was able to easily love my kids unconditionally and maybe a little too much at times. When it came to relationships, I was lost. I'm sure she had high hopes when she entered this relationship, (we all do).

MOVING FORWARD

SET GOALS TO be in relationships that you want your children to see because that's what they learn to accept from people who enter their lives. Children not only soak up what we say and do, they inherit our attitudes, bits and pieces of our personalities, and believe it or not a certain amount of our tolerance. If we show our children how a respectful relationship moves into a healthy marriage, they will expect a certain level of respect from their significant others. When they grow up in broken homes, they receive this information as acceptable and stay in unhealthy relationships that damaged their mental and at times physical state from those who could care less of the distress they are putting them through. As parents, we owe it to them to display compassion for other people, respect for people's feelings, and a healthy relationship without fragments of underlined hate.

I know it's easier said than done because we tell ourselves all the wrong things when we know we shouldn't be in a relationship. I think I've heard them all and even used the excuses myself. We usually say to ourselves, this person needs us in his or her life because he or she is the one for us. Or we convince ourselves that we can help this person, even though we see all the red flags from the beginning. No one wants to be alone, so we choose to stay until something better comes along. And then there's my favorite, when people simply stay because of the children. We're not doing ourselves a big favor by lying, but what we are doing is setting ourselves up to pursue a failed relationship. We're developing relationship habits off the fear of going through life alone.

I wouldn't recommend that someone stays in a relationship that goes against their morals, that they must cover up for their significant other's behavior, or for the well-being of their children. When people stay in relationships for their children, they are showing the children the worst side of who they can be as a mate and as a parent. When you're in a loveless relationship, it pulls you out of your personality so much so that the only thing your children will see is the damage *that* particular relationship has on you at the moment. If you don't want your children to go through what you went through, show them something different. Separate yourself from that destructive situation so your children can view you as a healthy, positive, happy, and loving person. Don't let them see you deteriorate into someone who's bitter, malicious, bad tempered, dishonorable, troublesome, or manipulative. You are the first role model they see growing up, they may adapt these negative traits and it will become difficult to reverse as time goes on. Tolerating an unhealthy relationship is not the way to cope simply because the American culture paints a family as a picture-perfect lifestyle. In today's world, it seems as if more and more people are choosing a single-family household. I'm glad my mother did, because it changed my life for the better.

For those who do not have children, think of your family. If you're with someone who mentally or physically abuses you, and you must cover for their behavior, they aren't for you. The person you should be protecting *this* person's actions from, is yourself. Don't let someone else's destructive, hostile, and ignoble thoughts or behavior cause you to alter your life and how you perceive love. As difficult as that may sound, you must always put you first because that's exactly what a negative person does. This is how he or she is able to hurt you in the way that they do. They are selfish and the only person that matters in *their* life is themselves, because they don't view you as something of value that they will eventually love. You are just a pond, a steppingstone until they can find someone else who they can tear down at an alarming rate.

Chapter Two

THE LESSONS LEARNED

IALWAYS SEEM TO ATTRACT individuals with charisma, there is something about them that makes me intrigued about who they are, where they come from, and where they may end up in life. This person was very mysterious to me; therefore, I took an interest. I was young and naïve, but my heart was open to new experiences. I decided to put my work before my personal life and a decision that would change the course of my life was made for me.

My mother would make dinner and call everyone to the kitchen, so we could make our plates. For some reason, every time we gathered into the kitchen to retrieve our meals, my brother would get sick. My mother was always one for bringing up those 'old myths' and said, "somebody is pregnant." It was between me and my sister-in-law and we both denied the accusation adamantly. My mother took me to the doctor the very next day, and lo and behold, I was the one with a child. When I went to go tell him that I was pregnant, he smiled and said he already knew. He admitted that he did it on purpose because he didn't want me to leave him behind as I pursued my career. I immediately saw him in a different light because I couldn't believe the lengths that someone would go through just to keep someone else in their life.

I was around 100 pounds and was very concerned about my figure, as most young girls are, so I wasn't eating as much as I should. I would receive a smack in the face and occasionally be locked in a closet. I thought these actions were warranted because of concern that I wasn't taking care of myself in the proper manner. I realized, that it wasn't that notion in the least bit that was causing these behaviors. Instead, it was a dissimilar way to administer pain without someone on the outside taking notice of control. I started to create distance to protect myself from any future abusive behavior. Needless to say, I picked up my eating habits and gained the proper weight for my size and age.

He was constantly out of town, which made it easier to become independently strong when it came to take on the responsibilities of a single teenage parent. When my son was born, he was notified, but came into town a month later. He called and asked to see my son, noting that he just got out of jail and wanted to bring him some diapers. I was alright with the visit, and after waiting for six hours decided to go to bed. He showed up at one in the morning knocking on my window. When I opened the front door, thinking he would request to see my son for the first time, he then asked me for money. Appalled, I close the door and walked back to my room heavy with disappointment. When I discussed the incident with my mother the next day she made a point to reiterate how strong I am and how I can handle this situation on my own.

A couple of months later I got a letter in the mail saying that my son had a sister, and they were a month apart in age. On one hand, I felt angry because he cheated on me and on the other I came to realize that this is the person he's been showing me from day one. He has always been selfish, and the fact that he got another teenage girl pregnant really took off the blinders for me. I started to develop a distaste for cheaters at this point in my life and for those who put themselves before others no matter how it leaves the other people in their path altered. Why was I so gullible to believe that when he was out of town visiting family, that he would ever be faithful to me? Why did it take me so long to understand that just because his words were saying he loved me, that his actions were really telling me the truth all along?

LOOKING BACK

Looking back on that relationship I realized, that not everyone who comes in your life, has the best intentions for you or the outcome of any decisions that they make while sharing this brief time with you. Knowing that I was involved with someone who was constantly in jail was disappointing to me because I was raised that you should be with someone who was of the same stature. If you live your life in a certain manner, your mate should also live life similar to your morals and values. That was a red flag that I ignored because I wanted to give him a chance to have an improved outlook on life.

Knowing what I know now, I feel as if I was way too trusting with this person and should take his behavior at face value. He was never going to change his habits for me just because I was pregnant and faithful. He was older than I was, so he had the upper hand when it came to life experience. As a teenager, I was living life free and had the entire world in my hands. My future was bright, I had everything going for me, and the only dim light in my life was him. I couldn't see it at the time, because a slap here and there was something that I took as "not too bad" compared to what I had witnessed as a child. But someone who hits you doesn't love you, and someone who mentally abuses you doesn't have your best interest at heart even if they say so.

Even though I had my son at a youthful age, I always made sure he had everything he needed and wanted for nothing at all. I finished school a year early, I worked hard, moved out of my mother's house, and provided a great life for him. The other person in this situation is nonexistent to us, he is an empty void in my son's life because he was never present enough for someone to develop a need for whatever he had to offer. In a way that's sad for my son, but I feel as if I've made up for any downfalls that this individual may have brought into my son's life. I'm not one of those individuals who bash the other parent, I just merely let their actions speak for themselves. My son is very capable of judging this person's character by the way he has displayed his actions over the years.

I believe I made the right decision by stepping up as both parents because I wouldn't want his injurious behavior to rub off on my son. Jail should not be a normal thing in one's life, it signifies that you are not or did not at one point in time, live your life in a manner to which your decisions were morally correct. Not wanting to expose something like that to my son, it was best that I remove this individual from our lives. This is not to confuse my decision to accept being a single parent with someone who withholds their child from the other parent because of personal, selfish, or vindictive reasons. He was always able to contact or visit my son, he just chose not to. Therefore, giving me a valid reason for moving forward with raising my son in the manner to which I feel puts him on the right path in life.

At some point, we all must grow up and accept the things that we've done in our past with the intent of developing personal growth. I realize that I was naïve, I understand that his cheating was not because of something that I said or did but stemmed from his own insecurities. I also know that I did the right thing by not exposing my son to someone who lives in a fashion to which his actions display narrowminded decision-making. Although this was my first taste of what it feels like to be cheated on by someone you trust, it hurt me more to know that my son was not someone who was considered a factor because this person was the one who purposely impregnated me. All of this started because he didn't want me to walk out of his life, but in the end, he eventually showed that that too was a lie and he couldn't even take responsibility in the choice he made for both of us. Which in turn, shattered my trust with anything else that he had to say after that point.

MOVING FORWARD

OUR TEENAGE YEARS are a time in our life when we are impressionable beyond belief. Although our parents can foresee some of the outcomes of our situations, we still decide to make the choice to press on anyway. Why should we take their advice, because they truly don't understand what we're going through at the time, right? If you are a teen who's reading this book, try to consider what your parents are telling you when they give you advice, (also known as) imposing on your life. They want the best for you and they don't want someone on the outside coming into your world, turning it upside down only to walk away unscathed while you sit there damaged. Your parents are the ones who are going to console you, brush you off, and send you back into the world brand-new again. They just want to make sure that you find someone who is going to give you less heartache than what you deserve.

If by chance you are in an abusive relationship or you know someone who is in an abusive relationship, the best thing for you, or for you to do for them, is to get out of that relationship. Don't accept someone's abuse or dishonesty because you let everyone after that person know, that you will be a steppingstone for them. It's best to learn at an early age not to tolerate someone else's egotistical needs. Don't ever enter someone's life displaying the fact you allow others to treat you in a way where you accept or tolerate abuse, to be cheated on, or to be talked down to at any given time. Make it known in the dating stage that you are against this behavior. By clearly stating and standing behind the fact that you don't condone physical abuse or cheating, it is most likely that that person will understand your valorous stance on the matter. If you leave the door open to chance, they will challenge and test you to see how far they can go before you walk away. Being headstrong from the beginning is an acceptable position for you to take because you ultimately began to get invested into a relationship and that sacrifice makes it harder for you to get out.

Be adamant about your convictions and who you want to share your life with. You don't owe anyone else your time just because you have it to give. Be with someone who not only values you as a person but who also wants the same things out of life so you both can move in the same direction. Take control of your life now so you can eliminate certain pains later in life. Learn to stand up for yourself and not be so accepting of other's lamentable behavior just because they sweet-talk you or give you material things. None of the things that they say or the gifts they give you will compensate for putting you in the hospital because of the physical damage they caused. None of it will matter when they're gone and you're still trying to mentally pick up the pieces so much so that you're damaging your current relationship. Don't allow someone the opportunity to make choices for you.

I knew all about protective sex and potential diseases at the time that I engaged in this exchange. I even protected myself by providing my own protection for him, but during the act, he decided to remove it unbeknownst to me, therefore, making the decision for the both of us. I learned at an early age that there are conniving people who would do just about anything in their power to control the situation you're in. Always be aware of who you're dealing with by getting to know them before you let them close enough to alter your life. My first mistake was not knowing him as well as I should have before engaging in sexual intercourse. If I would've taken the time to know him as an individual, I would've never got involved with someone who refuses to elevate past his personal situations. If I could've recognized early on that he was the type of person who had no intention of living a quality life, I may have saved myself the distress of getting convoluted.

When I see my son, I know that all my decisions are made because I put him first. I never let the fact of who that person was, destroy the man my son is today. Never put a significant other before your child because that person is capable of taking care of him or herself. Your children, on the other hand, need you as a responsible person to guide them in the right direction when steering them away from individuals who may potentially harm, cause mental suffering, and or afflict irreversible lacerations for which they carry with them throughout their life. Don't let your child wait for a parent who never shows up, don't allow someone to make promises to your child for which you know they will never keep. Be the voice for your child's disappointment when you make it clear to that person that if you didn't tolerate this type of inappropriate behavior in your life, you will not allow it to happen when it comes to the treatment of your child. Protect your children from harmful individuals with the intent of showing them how to recognize those who never take responsibility for their actions.

Chapter Three

AVOIDABLE

I WAS IN SEARCH OF SOMEONE who was more mature than my last relationship and was dead set on getting someone who was a bit older. I felt in my heart that I had grown into womanhood and someone who was slightly older than me would be a better fit. I quickly found out that just because someone is older than you in years, doesn't exactly mean that they are mature enough for you to build a future with. This guy was an oddball out, meaning, he wasn't in the in-crowd and he didn't quite fit in with the lost causes. I saw potential, so with that vision, I gave it a chance.

I didn't realize that this person was just ending a relationship to where he harbored insecurities from his past. He was adamant about starting a family and I was okay with that because I was seeking something permanent. I'm not the type of person to enter a short-term relationship and his vision of a future together appealed to me. I got pregnant with my son and instead of enjoying it, I realized that his attentiveness was not that at all, he was clingy because he thought I was going to cheat on him.

It didn't matter how many times I reassured him that I was not his ex-girlfriends, he continued to treat me as if there was someone else that

I was hiding. The constant accusations made me not want to be around him and I began to throw myself into work just to avoid confrontation. We begin to physically fight at least once a week and argue daily and this is something that my children witnessed or heard after being sent to their room. If possible, I tried not to have disputes with anyone while they were around, but kids are smart and I'm pretty sure they knew what was going on at the time. Nevertheless, it didn't sit well with me and I decided that the best thing for me to do was to pack up my kids and leave the relationship. Receiving disagreement with my plans, that decision resulted in the first time I was literally put through a wall.

I knew right then and there that the relationship was over, and I was done paying for someone else's mistakes. It seems as if the unresolved issues he carried with him from his past relationships would not allow him to focus on his current situation. Because he viewed his past as worthless, anything that he tried to build without first addressing those issues would fail. I felt as if there was nothing that I could do to help him because his mind was already made up. No matter how many times I tried to rationalize his theory, I could never convince him that I wasn't cheating. I would allow him to have access to everything that I had just to ease his mind on the topic and he would still come back with accusations a couple of days later. I was fighting a losing battle and frankly, I was tired.

There was nothing else that I could do to put his mind at ease and as soon as I got the opportunity to do so, I left. It was better for me to walk away from that situation even though I felt guilty about leaving him to deal with his issues alone. Then I got a phone call that instantly deleted all that guilt. The woman on the other end let me know that she too had a son with this man. All that time he was accusing me of cheating when he was the one with someone else. Not only was he with someone else, but they had a baby together. She said after I broke it off, her relationship turned volatile because she was not me. I felt bad for her because she didn't deserve that type of abuse from someone who didn't appreciate or value who she was as an individual. I washed my hands with the whole situation and moved forward with my life. I can only assume that he did the same, seeing that he never made an effort to see my son again. Maybe he came to the realization that he could not look my son in the face knowing what he had put us through. Then too, it's possible that he just didn't care enough to mend any of his wrongdoings because it's much easier to move on to the next unsuspecting person who will believe and trust what you tell them without question.

LOOKING BACK

THIS PERSON WAS ultimately damaged goods and was projecting his issues on to me as if I was the one who committed these horrible sins against him. I felt bad about what his ex-girlfriend/s had put him through and wanted to genuinely be there for him. I was young back then and always thought I could save someone from something. As I got older, I realized that it's not my job to save those who don't want to be saved. To this day, I am unsure if he ever had cheating girlfriends in his past, or if that is something that he was just telling me in order to be the one cheating. Life has a funny way of twisting things when you're not ready for them, and I was blinded by being a positive person in his life when in hindsight I should've been questioning why he was *so* adamant about me not being honest.

It was very difficult to pay for someone else's mistakes if they actually happened and affected him like he said they did. It's even worse to pay for someone else's mistakes if they were a made-up story just so he could get away with blindsiding me with his cheating antics. When I found out that he was seeing someone else and she already had his son, it made me realize that I allowed this individual to manipulate my kindness with the intent of being unfaithful. It was sickening and although I felt sorry for her because she was still in the situation, I didn't feel bad for anything that he had coming his way. How could he make me believe that he despised cheaters when he was actually the one cheating? It's crazy for me to sit back and think about it because I never suspected that he was that type of person.

This situation made me become aware of those who try to make me pay for mistakes that aren't ultimately mine. If I didn't cheat, don't make me out to be a cheater in your head. It was up to him to deal with his insecurities before he entered into a new relationship, and that's something that he never took the time out to accomplish. I spent most of my time in that situation proving to him that I was worthy and was nothing like these ex-girlfriends. I feft like I wasted so much time on the topic of cheating when I did nothing wrong. That time should've been spent growing the relationship and not wasted on his mental past. The real investment should've been on why he chose to shine a light on being faithful when he was the one cheating with someone else.

I can only speculate at this point because it happened years ago, but I learned not to believe any and everything that comes out of someone's mouth because they could be sending me on a wild goose chase. He certainly did, and the only way that I found out about it was because he was physically abusing the other lady. When she told me that her relationship turned physical because she wasn't me, it struck a chord and made me want to help her out of the situation. I believe that's just a part of my personality, helping others, especially when I perceive them as the underdog in a situation. I do have to say, it opened my eyes to realize that no matter what someone says, I had to become a better judge of character.

I must rationalize what people tell me because even though it sounds like they need me, it could just be another form of manipulation. I don't like to participate in someone else's song and dance, therefore it's up to me to decide whether I want to play a part in someone else's story. I learned to make my own rules as I go along in any relationship and continue to exist in that partnership how I see fit. I no longer leave it up to the other person to write up a part for me in their life. It's up to me to portray myself as the woman I am and let the other person work around my characteristics. I feel like I gave too much of myself in this relationship to help someone's mental state reach a balance of acceptance. I was wrong in doing so and from this point on, found that it's best for me to walk my truth while they find who they are along the way. It's not my job or responsibility to fix previous issues from past relationships that I wasn't involved in.

MOVING FORWARD

Don't let others capitalize on your characteristics. Conniving people see those who are kindhearted, in need of something, sympathetic to certain situations, and understanding without question. They prey on those who have mercy because in the end, they need that bleeding heart to cover up the negativity that they bring into the relationship. Always be aware of a person who is doing way too much and trying way too hard to make you believe them over what your instincts are telling you. There's a reason why a mate gets dramatic when called out in certain situations. There is a reason why that person tries to flip the script and make everything else your fault when that's not even the topic at hand. There's a reason why this person must convince you to believe in their antics and it's not because they're telling the truth. Learn to listen to that voice in your head because it's there for your own protection.

The time that we have on this earth goes by so fast and it's a shame when someone enters your life and decides to waste or play with that time. If you think back to all the people that wasted your time; I'm sure there were better things that you could have been doing with those years shared with someone else who valued the time you spent together. I know we can't change the past, although some of us would like to, we can learn how to shape our future by learning from the relationships we encounter. I try to look at every relationship as a lesson and not wasted time, simply because I've learned something from each of them. I've acquired information along the way that would assist me in determining what not to do or applying what works for me in future relationships. This is not to say that I don't think I would've rather been doing something substantial with my life than learning these lessons from people who didn't deserve to share my time. Although, it does solidify the fact that if I didn't go through my past the way that it happened, I may be learning these lessons too late in life to reap the benefits of the experience.

Everyone in life has an agenda, whether it's disruptive or beneficial to your life is the choice that you must make when choosing a partner. Should we have to question everyone's motives? As a young person, I would've said no to that question. As someone wiser in my years, I say yes, especially if you have children. It's one thing to make a choice to share your life with a mate and deal with his or her antics, but you must question if said antics will leave an impression on your children. I encourage everyone to study a potential partner's motives. A person's representative can only play the part for so long before their true colors step into the light. If this person is meant to be in your life, take your time and examine their patterns, personality traits, and triggers. I'm not saying scrutinize their every move and investigate everything that comes out of their mouth. I'm just saying don't ignore the red flags because every canvas is not blank. There's always an underlined motive.

Ponder over what you want from this person, consider the outcome if you begin to accept his or her negativity. How far will this person go to drain you of every ounce of good you have left before you begin to consume their destructive, harmful, and damaging behavior as your own? If you're a happy-go-lucky person, don't let someone else's negative mental state impede on your characteristics so in turn, you adapt their undesirable ways. In other words, don't allow someone else's inhospitable demeanor to control the direction of your life. Whatever past issues a person has does not concern you because you in no way shape or form embedded these problems into their head. Someone who manipulates is not a partner worth sharing life with because you never know if they mean well.

Chapter Four

THE ANTICS

I WANTED SOMETHING FUN, exciting, and eventful in my next relationship. In the beginning, I had such an enjoyable time and this person was interested in one of my favorite pastimes thus, I just knew it would work out this time. I was wrong because I chose to ignore all the signs that said we were incompatible. I was a single mother who always spoiled my kids with the latest of gadgets, clothes, and toys. They never wanted for anything and I believe that this person wanted someone in his life to overindulge him the way I did with my children. I am naturally a giver and coming out of a failed relationship with an older person, it was a step in a different direction to have someone closer to my age who I could share my world without restrictions.

    I thought I was helping someone who came from a very rough upbringing with seeing the world through a more improved lifestyle. I worked a lot of hours at my job but was paid very well and he benefited from the fruits of my labor after he moved in with me. He got very comfortable and eventually left his job, leaving me with the sole responsibility of providing for him. I didn't mind in the beginning because he opted to take care of my children which in turn allowed me to work more than ever. I was happy with the arrangement until I noticed less and less of an effort on his part. He began to feed me excuses of why it was inconvenient for him to watch the kids because he had plans or other obligations that needed to be fulfilled. Being the mother that I am, I made other arrangements for my children, so I would not have to reduce my workload. This left him free of all responsibility and I no longer looked at him as someone who was beneficial to the relationship but more of a third child.

Once the blinders were removed, I ended up finding out he was too immature for the type of relationship I was seeking at the time. After I would get off work, I would pick up my children, and walk into my home to see him and his friends playing video games. One of the gentlemen let me know that this is something they do daily and that changed my whole outlook on having him as a mate. Here I am working nonstop, taking care of my children, cleaning my home, cooking dinner, getting my children ready for school, and preparing myself for the next workday, only to have the routine continue throughout the week. Then there's him, still in bed when we're leaving for the day, inviting his friends over for game sessions, eating everything in sight, and staying up all hours of the night. This is not what I envisioned my situation to become when I agreed to share my life with someone I was interested in.

I set him down and voiced the fact that I was unhappy with how things turned out and he needed to either find some employment and start engaging with what's going on in our situation or he could exit the relationship with no love lost. He decided to stay in the relationship and get focused on a career move. Soon after that decision I became pregnant and thought things would work out. I was wrong again because during my pregnancy one of his friends clued me in on the fact that he was cheating. I knew this friend was interested in me, so I didn't believe him. One night I was a designated driver for my friends and the same person asked me to take a ride with him because my mate needed me. I drove with the friend in my car, who gave me directions to a house I'd never been to. He honked the horn, and my mate came out of the front door with his shirt in his hand and buckling up his pants. I was instantly filled with rage as I backed out of the driveway and sped off.

I returned myself and the friend back to the establishment where we begin this little adventure and explained to my friends that I was leaving for the night. While I was exiting the parking lot, my mate ran over to the car, jumped in, and immediately started to explain himself. It was nothing that I wanted to hear because I was already focused on the excruciating pain I was feeling in my stomach. I drove myself to the hospital and entered the emergency room explaining to the lady at the front desk what I was experiencing. She asked me to sit down and she would have someone with me in a moment. I went to the bathroom and he was hot on my trail still trying to explain himself outside of the door. I opened the door and yell at him to get the nurse because something was wrong. She came into the bathroom, checked me down below, looked me in my face, and told me not to push. 30 seconds later she came back for me and I was placed on a bed and wheeled to an elevator where they began to hook up an IV and provide oxygen. All the while, the cheater was kissing my forehead asking for forgiveness cause he wanted to be in his baby's life!! I went straight into the operating room where the doctor told me that my baby was coming right now. I told him that that was impossible because I was only six months pregnant. Nevertheless, he coached me to push and I did so. I felt what I thought was my baby coming into the world, but I didn't hear any crying. The doctor explained to me that the placenta and all the fluid came out, but my baby was still inside. They would have to do an emergency cesarean section. From that point, they knocked me out.

When I came to, it was so I could see my baby for the first time before he was airlifted to a children's ward at another hospital. He was in the incubator as he opened his eyes and looked at me, and they knocked me out again. They only woke me up to get permission over the phone for the surgery he was going through as he was fighting for his life. Because he was born early, his lungs weren't fully developed, and he needed a few blood transfusions. My mother and family went to be by his side, therefore he could have a support system and wouldn't be alone. The doctors also said they see a lot of improvement with human contact, remarkably my mother made sure to be his personal masseuse by rubbing his hand/

back, providing him with kisses, and being that soothing voice, he needed to pull through. When I came to and saw my mother and a woman I never met before sitting at the foot of my bed, I already knew. I started to tear up and my mother didn't say a word, she just climbed on the bed with me and she whispered in my ear "I'm sorry, he fought as long as he could, but he didn't make it." I buried my son because of this person's incapability of being faithful.

I was in a very vulnerable state and he kept feeding me the notion of how improved our relationship was going to be. Because of the tragedy I experienced, it was eye-opening! He vowed to be the man I needed because he owed it to me. This was his way of taking fault of what happened to my son. He felt (in his mind) that he could make up for the fact that I lost my son by finally stepping up to help around the house, be more involved with the children, and getting a job. A part of me wanted to believe him simply because I know people can change, but that didn't happen in this case. I started to resent him and developed a distaste for him as a person. I made him sleep on the couch and refused to acknowledge that he even existed in the home. I took my power back and the dynamic of the relationship changed severely. Arguments begin to happen more than ever and physical altercations became an often occurrence. During an argument, he informed me of all the women he cheated on me with and the fact that he named some of these affairs after my son's funeral was what sealed his fate.

LOOKING BACK

Looking back on this relationship, I can see that it was very toxic. There was a lot of cheating on his part and that's never good for any relationship. Anyone who cheats is not truly invested in the relationship they're pretending to belong to. I can never take someone seriously who spreads himself out to multiple partners because he's too focused on everything else to truly consume any type of love or affection that I could give him. Because he had way too much going on to give me 100% of who he was as a person, I'll never truly know who he was. I had a feeling that he was cheating but I never had proof so there was nothing that I could confront him about. After the fact, another one of his friends filled in the missing pieces for me. He explained that when my children and I were away for the day, that's when he would go off to meet up with other girls and then be back home with his friends before I was off work. That way everyone was already settled in with snacks and gameplaying, consequently seeming as if they had been there all day. You can't fall in love at contrasting times in a relationship and think it'll work out. I was into this individual before and he treated me like he could do anything he wanted because he knew I would be there. I got tired of his negative, dishonest, and toxic behavior and started to despise him as a person. I began to drop my feelings by creating distance and it was then that he started to fall for me. It was too late because I'd already had enough and couldn't forgive the damage that was already done.

I guess his cheating was something to be expected for a young guy who was away from home for the first time and needed a home life but was incapable of being anything but one of the children. The cheating made me see that I could never change someone's need to run around with other women. At that point in my life, I vowed that I would never return to someone who cheated on me because I was ultimately giving that person a pass to cheat again. He showed me how it felt to be mistreated, I then, in turn, reversed the dynamics on him until I broke his spirit. I didn't cheat, but I made sure that he understood that his actions were no longer going to be tolerated in my home or against me moving forward. Knowing I had my power back, made me ruthless to anyone who attempted to cross me from that point on. Just because I was the woman in the relationship didn't mean that I had to be passive, it didn't mean that I had to take unnecessary heartache from someone who wasn't even worth my time. He didn't value me enough to consider that his antics may cause me to lose my son and the memories that my son and I could've had along with the joy he could've brought to those who loved him.

My partner should not be equal to my children and I believe this is the role he thought he should play instead of being someone who stood by my side. I was simply trying to elevate the cultural aspect of his life and he took that to be somewhat mother-some. He was young, immature, unfaithful, and I expected too much so I could never be fulfilled by anything he did because he constantly let me down. I can't depend on someone who is undependable and that was my issue. I should've just accepted the fact that he was way too immature to step into a family situation and take on the responsibilities of an already made household. Looking back on this relationship, I realize that this is when I decided, once I have it in my head that I'm done with the situation or person, there's no forgiving or giving a second chance. Why wait to see when/if this person is going to make me regret giving that option to someone when they had it in the first place? I no longer believe in second chances because the first chance that you get is the *only* chance that you have to make it right. Why should I subject myself to someone else's foolishness because they choose to play with my heart, my feelings, and my time? I should never have to hear someone say, 'give me another chance' because he threw away the chance he already had. We only get one chance in life, why should I allow you more than the next person who has the same opportunity to get it right the first time?

After losing my son, I began to turn the tables from being the victim and started to be the predator. I only changed the way that I lived my life, so I can be ready for any potential shenanigans. It's not because of his dishonesty that I changed my life, it's just that he, in turn, made me want to take notice of things that I took for granted, which was freedom! The right to be me without any restrictions! Through and through, the pain was unbearable and over the years I learned how to work on myself as a woman. A woman should always carry herself with sophistication in mind. Most think that respect should be demanded so they demand it. In retrospect, respect is earned, therefore when a woman acquires respect, she should do so with a refinement mindset.

Ultimately a woman's respect paints a picture of her personality. She should always carry herself in a high-class manner with the intent of receiving the respect of a high-class woman. How we carry ourselves as women reflect the respect we should receive not only from our partners but from anyone gifted with the worldview to notice the difference between sophistication and immaturity. I will never allow someone to take advantage of me while I'm in a vulnerable state and get away with their behavior by entertaining their actions for another day. Promises don't last long when a person conveniently benefits from a low point in your life. Once you are made whole again, you either lash out, or you walk away. I must respect myself enough to walk away, so *that* individual knows I am not to tolerate any of his manipulative negotiations.

MOVING FORWARD

IF YOU ARE EVER in the position financially or emotionally to enhance someone's life, do so with caution. Make sure that that person understands that you are his or her mate and that a parental figure is not something that you wish to become. It is imperative to separate the two when looking for someone that you want to share the rest of your life with, that way you don't get set into a role that you are not prepared to take on because your kindness was intended to uplift this individual as a person. As funny as that may seem to some of you, it happens. I tried to elevate this person's life by inspiring him to become a better individual and it backfired on me because I wasn't crystal clear about my intentions to inspire and not to take on a burden. I, in no way, shape, or form intended for him to become complacent with my lifestyle so much so that he was content with not growing as an individual. He became stagnant and that was unattractive to me and where I begin to lose respect for him.

When someone decides to cheat on you, they make the decision for the both of you on how things are going to turn out in your relationship. I don't condone cheating whatsoever, I truly believe that if there is someone else that catches your eye when you are in a relationship, you should end your current relationship before moving on to something/one new. I'm not saying that this should happen because someone winked at you, I'm simply saying that if you are willing to lie about your whereabouts, hide or erase any type of communication with someone you're interested in, or physically get involved with someone other than your partner, you should end your current relationship to spare your mate the heartache and yourself the embarrassment of becoming a cheater. Don't string someone along just because you're good at keeping them in the dark, that's a cowardly act. Face the fact that you are not happy and have a conversation with your mate explaining why. You may be able to come together and mend what's left of your relationship without you hurting other individuals in the process with your selfishness.

Losing a child is very difficult and some will never get over those emotions (I haven't). Make sure that you never allow someone to interfere with you bringing a healthy child into the world. If you have a cheating mate, and you're pregnant, get out of that situation right away. When you realize that someone is unfaithful to you, it affects your emotional state which causes stress. Some people fall into a state of depression, some people get angry and cheat just because their mate is cheating, and others leave the relationship as soon as they find out about the infidelity. Don't do like I did in this situation and wait until I have proof to confront someone about what I already know in my heart is true. Once I had the proof, it was too late and the stress of it all landed me in the hospital having my son prematurely. I almost didn't make it to my son's funeral because they wouldn't release me from the hospital until I broke my fever which lasted a few days. I think it's absurd when someone cheats on a pregnant wife or girlfriend, I cannot stress enough on how important it is for women to have a calm and stress-free pregnancy.

Relationships can ultimately change who you are as an individual. Take me for example, I entered this relationship thinking I was doing a good thing for someone who I thought at the time was deserving. By the end of the relationship, I developed a thick skin because I was put through so many changes that the only way I would walk away with my head held high was if I became a hardened person. I had to learn how to deal with someone else's selfishness when it came to matters of the heart. Don't constantly let someone's inconsiderate ways interfere with who you are so much so that you lose the person you entered the relationship as just to leave as a crushed soul. Always maintain the person that you are because that insight is what will continue to guide you to the way things are supposed to be. I say this because I don't want you to be unconcerned with your needs and wants because someone else has put it in your head that they should be the one who comes first. Don't believe for one moment that their happiness means more than your happiness, or their needs are more important than your needs. If you remain confident that there is a certain type of love that you deserve, you will recognize that there are certain things an egotistical person cannot get past you. Take care of yourself first so you can always remain standing tall because no matter what you go through in a relationship, it's your responsibility to survive.

Chapter Five

IMPROVISED

PERSONALITY WISE, THIS individual and I were compatible, to say the least. We were enjoying life at the beginning of an era that changed my take on living life on the edge. He was someone who loved my children and made an effort to go out of his way to make them feel like they were a part of his life. We related to one another's past when it came to family and what we wanted moving forward. We both came from a single parent home, had strong mothers who set ambitious standards, and a small number of immediate family members who we could depend on. He was a responsible person who was genuinely there for me and I was seeking a loyal mate at that time in my life. I trusted in our union so much so, that we begin discussing the expansion of our family unit.

After trying for a few months, we were both excited to hear that I was pregnant and took all the necessary precautions to make sure my pregnancy would be a healthy one. Everything had been well, and I was going in to get a routine ultrasound when the tech excused herself from the room. She came back in and said she had spoken with my doctor who wanted me to meet him at his office as soon as possible with the results. Thinking nothing of it, I went to his office and was immediately put into a room to see him. I was moved to another room and just assumed that it was because I didn't have an appointment and they were seeing those who were on the schedule that day. It was getting close to closing time and he finally came in and explained to me that I was purposely put in a room, so I would not leave. Confused I asked why and that is when he informed me that my ultrasound didn't go so well. The tech didn't see my baby in my uterus and when he looked at the ultrasound, he saw that my baby was in my fallopian tube.

He had already reserved an operating room and we needed to go in for an emergency tubal ligation to remove the baby. I was stunned when he told me that the baby was big enough to erupt my fallopian tube and I would have died over the weekend. I agreed that it was necessary to have surgery right away and so went my normal day at the doctor that ended a wanted pregnancy. I was released the next day and I went home but had complications passing urine. I had the urge to go, but it just burned so badly inside. I went back to my doctor for a follow-up and my mate informed the doctor that I hadn't been going to the bathroom. After examining and running tests for most of the day, the doctor inserted a catheter and I was put on bed rest because of an infection which occurred because of the surgery. I had a urine bag attached to myself, stuck in bed, and the only thing I could think about was my children. During the day; my mate took care of all my needs and when the kids came home from school, he made sure they too had everything they needed and put them to bed.

We moved past that tough time in our lives and began a new chapter that would bring on way more stress than either of us could handle. Because he took a break from his job to take care of me, when it came time to return, he decided that he was going to abandon his career choice. He had gotten too comfortable and I began taking care of two extra able-bodied individuals who weren't contributing to the household we all shared. I say two because one of our friends were going through a challenging time and moved in with us. I had already had my fill of taking care of someone who had the ability to support himself and after a few months of supporting and cleaning up after this situation, I began to create distance.

Here I was doing everything in my power to make sure that the rent was paid, the lights were turned on, we all had food to eat, and I wasn't getting any help from the two people who could've made this situation a lot better. As my mate, I felt as if he let me down because he made the choice to just check out of life and leave me to handle any and everything that came my way. As an adult who has children, I didn't have the option to take time off from my job as a parent because I needed a break. I didn't feel as if he should have the option to take time off being a part of the family either, but from my point of view, it seemed as if he went on a permanent vacation. I no longer viewed him as my partner in crime, I now saw him as an extra being who I was now responsible for. It took some time, but we both agreed that we should call it quits so we wouldn't end on bad terms. It was for the best because we remained friends afterward.

LOOKING BACK

It's always a plus when you enter a relationship with someone who has a great personality. Knowing that there is a common goal that the both of you are shooting for is always a positive in a relationship. This individual is caring, and he always puts others first. The relationship was not volatile at all and that gave us the ability to focus on living life in a manner that would help us grow together and as individuals when the time came to separate. Unfortunately, somewhere in the relationship, he became a friend instead of a significant other. I don't hold any ill will toward things that happened in the past because he felt as if he was doing what was best for him at the time. Who am I to take away from his decision when it was something that he obviously felt needed to be done for his own sanity.

The only thing I could do for him was to be a supportive mate, and I did that for as long as I could without damaging everything that we worked on from the beginning. He was not moving forward and that is something that I needed him to do especially when setting an example of what a man is supposed to do when he is being looked at through the eyes of my children. I don't want them to think that it's alright to check out and not mentally return to those who depend on you. It's an awkward thing to explain to your children as to what's going on when they ask about the actions of someone else who has totally done a turnaround from the person they once knew to be strong and full of answers. To combat this, I made it a point to get the children out of the house as much as possible, so their minds weren't on the havoc that was caused by this person's decision to leave his job and endure the consequences.

If it wasn't for the desertion of his career, I believe that the relationship would have gone in a better direction with positive results. This is one of those times that you just wonder because there isn't a right or wrong answer for what could've been. As healthy as this relationship started out, it is true that finances can damage something good. Am I not saying that that is the single reason why we didn't work out? Absolutely not, finances had a significant amount to do with the breakup because I believe that if I had the money to support a household of five individuals with no problem at all, the fact that he remained stagnant would've eventually taken a toll on me. The only difference is, it would have taken much longer for me to develop those type of feelings. In retrospect, I'm glad things happen the way they did because we were able to salvage a friendship.

The thing that I took away from this relationship the most was the fact that you can have a friendship with one of your ex-mates without there being any type of romantic or sexual feeling at all. He can call and talk to me about anything and I have no problem being there for him because I know I will get the same thing in return if needed on my end. After everything was said and done, we had the ability to discuss where things went wrong and how it made us into better people because of it. It's always good to know that we learn and grow from those who cross our paths without tainting the reason why we were brought together in the first place. Even when reminiscing about the good times shared, we can always laugh and make things right. That's what relationships are about, being able to have the opportunity to get to know someone who has good intentions and come out on the other end of that relationship with lessons learned.

MOVING FORWARD

When your partner becomes your roommate, it is truly a key sign that it's time to walk away from that relationship. I understand that it is difficult to imagine being without someone because of the time that you have invested into a relationship with him or her, but it's in both of your best interests to end it before things turn ugly. When that happens, it's even more difficult to get back on a common ground enough for you to even communicate without losing your cool or belittling the other person. You should never walk around with that much built up anger that manifests over someone that you had deep feelings for or even loved at one point in time in your life. Learn to forgive that individual for things that happened in the past, so you have the capability of looking forward. If you keep living in that era of your life, you will never have the skill to invest in your present relationship with the intention of building a substantial future. In other words, it's up to you to grow past damaging or hurtful situations that have occurred in your life so that you can become a person of significance when it's time for you to focus, submerge into, and dedicate yourself to someone new.

Regardless of what you put into the relationship, when one person checks out, it's not your responsibility to pick up the pieces because they have no intentions of making the effort to change the situation. That person has literally told you and is now showing you through his or her behavior that they are no longer able or willing to fight for the life of your relationship. They may be there physically, romantically, and even offer some form of help around the home, but they have ultimately made the decision to put him or herself first. The only time that this is ever condoned, is if this individual is suffering from some sort of mental breakdown, a sickness, or a disease of some sort. Then it's up to you as a partner to make sure that he or she gets the medical or mental treatment he or she needs. Other than that, it is not okay for a mate to bail out on the relationship and leave you with every responsibility that you both agreed to share. There must be progress from both parties involved when it comes to growing the relationship. Don't allow someone to take your kindness for weakness because it will eat at you until your feelings become numb and you will mentally place this person back into the friend zone.

Don't let someone's lack of motivation impede on your journey because they've become so comfortable with the lifestyle you share that they forget that that comfort comes from work on both of your parts. They must put in the same amount of effort as you to get the happiness, the affection that develops from being attentive, and the willingness to want to cater to one's needs because of what transpires from being loved. No one just shows up and gets the world handed to them when they haven't done anything in return to make the other person feel the way they do inside. Your representative never informs your new mate, that once things start going well, you will opt out and ultimately leave them to figure out how everyone else is going to live. No way, your representative shows up to be the person you make them want to not live without.

Represent your true self from the beginning and you never have to worry about facing those tough times that life throws at you alone, because your mate will always be willing to take the lead until you're fully capable of jumping back in the game.

Chapter Six

THE SPONTANEITY

HE WAS CHARMING IN THE way he carried himself and made it a point to be real at all times. He was something new and different from other mates I had endured. I can **genuinely say, he was a** breath of fresh air and the fact that he didn't play video games was more than a plus for me. We enjoyed music and we shared a lot of good times just being in one another's presence. I am a lover of movies and he was also and having that in common expanded our conversations as we would always have an opinion of how things went or how different they could've been if said characters were in different genres. It didn't bother me that he was younger than I was because this person was wise beyond his years. I almost looked at him as an old soul because he was well put together and had a certain je ne sais quoi that naturally attracted others to him.

He enjoyed being around my children and he taught them how to carry themselves with respect when it came to being challenged by an outsider. They would have eating contests with almost any type of food with a man versus food theme. New Year's Eve and the fourth of July was always exciting because he made sure to have an abundant number of fireworks that he popped off for the kids. As a comedian at heart, the time spent with the children was enjoyable because he wanted to be seen as more of a friend and less of a father figure. That was a smart choice at that time in their lives because there was no pressure of being someone in their head who he would never amount to because he wasn't who they imagined.

His job sent him away for a very long time, but my life continued as I had to support my children and take care of the household. I tossed myself into my work which caused me to travel and be away from home for weeks at a time. We grew closer in our newfound long-distance relationship and when he returned home, we picked up where we left off without skipping a beat. I, on the other hand, continued to work just as much as I did when he left because it was what I was focused on at the time. When he was away, he was on a different schedule, so he would be wide-awake while everyone else was asleep. During those times he would be online chatting with various strangers, I didn't think anything of it because I too was in chat rooms to pass the time.

I wanted to surprise him by coming home early from a trip and had it all planned out in my head. I am most definitely the master when it comes to spoiling someone with a great time, it reflects my appreciation for sharing life with me. He was at work when I arrived and left up a private conversation he was having with a young lady outside of a chat room. I read it and was very shocked at the content and questions she was asking but blew it off because his answers were matter-of-fact, and it looked like he was keeping the conversation at bay and steering it away from something distasteful. When he got home, he was excited to see me and begin to get ready, so I could take him out for a night on the town.

I invited another couple to accompany us and we were waiting for them to call so we could meet up at a certain time to take one vehicle to the event. I answered the phone and it was not our friends, but the young lady from the Internet. She informed me that it was her birthday and he was supposed to meet up with her to deliver her birthday present and some money. I was very calm in this conversation and politely informed her that I was his significant other, the financial breadwinner, and the owner of all vehicles parked at the home. She kindly let me know that they met once before and described the car that he took her in to get dinner and to see a movie. She assured me that nothing went on past that and she would not be contacting him any longer. I, in turn, assured her that if she wanted him, I could drop him off along with his five children at her dwelling, but would be cutting off all funds and leaving him without a car. She said that wasn't quite in her plans and she would be moving on from there. I embellished to make him seem less attractive, he didn't have any kids at all, but since he started being dishonest, I didn't see any reason for me to paint him as a good catch. Needless to say, I called the friends, canceled the evening, and kicked him out.

That was the first time I ever seen him cry, but he gathered up all his things and placed them in his vehicle. My response was very cold because I truly expected better from him and I didn't want him to see me sweat. He stood in the doorway of the home and I told him to leave his keys on the table and I went to my room. I heard the front door close and like most people in that position, I started to question everything else that may have happened leading up to that point. I was in no mood to cook dinner, so I ordered out, fed my children, and put them to bed. After watching a movie in my room, I came out to get a drink (I really needed one). I heard what sounded like a TV coming from the front of the house, so I grabbed my gun and went to investigate. I noticed a light coming from my spare room and when I slowly opened the door I could see a figure (that clearly was not one of my children) laying in the bed! As I moved closer, gun drawn, I realized it was my newly ex-mate. Relieved that it wasn't a stranger, I woke him up and we talked for most of the night.

I forgave him because he explained that he wanted to come back to the relationship that he had before his job sent him away. With me working constantly and away from home, he reached out to people on the Internet because he was lonely. He said that it wouldn't have gone any further than hanging out because to him she was a temporary replacement for myself. Did I truly believe this? No, but because I know he had been through a lot with his job and it put a strain on our relationship I felt at least I owed it to him to take partial blame because I never slowed down when he returned. I could see how he felt because I didn't take time to invest back into the relationship, and for that reason alone we moved forward.

Lo and behold his job sent him away two months later for an extended amount of time. I dove right back into my work, but this time when he returned I took off work for a month to rekindle and solidify our home life. There was a new issue that arose as he began to display signs of PTSD. When I asked him to seek help, he informed me that he didn't want a blemish on his record, because reporting PTSD could possibly hurt him from furthering his next career. He left that job and as we discussed, he took some time off to clear his head. I went back to work because now I was the sole breadwinner of the household, which was fine because he had his own money in savings. His sleeping was off just like the first time and he began to accumulate things that didn't belong to him, threaten bystanders, and harm himself physically. He refused to get the help he needed and that left me with only one option, it was time to walk away.

LOOKING BACK

LOOKING BACK ON this relationship I had a lot of enjoyable and memorable times. I was very happy in the relationship and although I was growing as a person by investing time in myself and improving my career, something was missing. All of our friends looked at us as the model couple and wanted what we had, but what we shared wasn't perfect by far. Miscommunication of our needs set us back from the first time he went away. What we should have done was sat down and discussed our game plan about how we were going to handle him leaving and his returns. The thing about that is, when he left the first time, it was something that neither of us ever experienced in a relationship. With that said I feel as if there was no way around it because it was water not yet treaded. I think the situation would've gone in a different direction if he could've conveyed the notion that he wanted a warm homecoming to me before he left his destination. I would've made the necessary arrangements with my job, so I could be there, and he wouldn't have felt lonely enough to reach out to a stranger and almost lose everything that he had been craving while he was away.

I am not saying that it's all his fault because things happened the way they did, I am just saying if we had an open line of communication by taking notes from other couples who had been through the same thing we had been through, things would've been a little more positive. I am a strong entity just like I thought he was a strong entity and together we didn't want to disturb the other by expressing our needs. I needed to continue to work as much and as hard as I did because I was on a roll and I didn't want to stop that for fear that I couldn't pick up where I left off if I interfered with how well I was doing. To make up for me being gone, I just threw money at the situation and he seemed happy. He clearly needed me to be home until he was able to adjust back to his home life but didn't want to tell me to slow down because he saw how happy it made me.

I felt as if I couldn't help him past the mental issues he was facing. I made my decision to walk away because my children were involved, and as a parent, it's up to me to keep them safe. They were sheltered from a lot of his activity but witnessed some of his shenanigans when strange things would just pop up in our home that wasn't there when they went to bed the night before. Oddly enough, sometimes he wouldn't even remember going out in the middle of the night and collecting these things. It was not my place to inform my children of this person's mental state, but I began to get worried for their safety when I was away at work. It was very hard for me to concentrate when something like that was always in the back of my mind. Whenever one of my kids would call me, my heart would drop to the floor because my first thought is, something happened involving my mate. I couldn't live like that any longer and it was in the best interest of us all to separate.

My children and I have nothing but good things to say about this person because he was entertaining and always up to something. He made you sit down and really think about things that mattered in life.

He would go into deep conversations and question just about anything that regular people took for granted. And he always had these little sayings of knowledge that he would spit out at precise times, so they would make sense and compel the conversation into a more complex dimension. He was never one who belittled an individual because of their lack of knowledge on a certain topic, he would just kindly inform them of the information needed in a joking manner, so they won't feel ignorant about the subject. There was a lot of good times with this one, I wish him well wherever he is in life.

MOVING FORWARD

First and foremost, never put your children in the care of someone who is unhealthy, to the point where you question their ability to keep your kids safe. That was my biggest mistake and one that I never repeated after the fact. It doesn't matter how much you love someone and know that they have goodness in their heart, that love will never trump a mental illness. And it isn't worth risking that something may or may not happen to your children when you are away. I assure you, it will drive you crazy every single time this individual is alone with your children and is supposed to be the responsible adult.

It's the same concept when someone is using drugs or is an alcoholic, they can never be trusted to babysit children because you never know what the outcome will be when you return to retrieve your kids. I trusted, hoped, and prayed that nothing would happen to my children, but I always had that little voice in my head so when I was gone for a few days at a time, they would stay with my mother. It was better for me to know that their surroundings were safe, so I didn't have to worry about him having a dream or a flashback and not snapping out of it before the damage was done. It's always better to be safe than sorry, especially in a situation of denial.

Denial of the fact that help is needed by the person who needs it the most never moves in a healthy direction. If the type of help a person needs is offered through the workplace, take it. Sometimes, an individual needs to be given an ultimatum to receive the help that he or she needs. That might be the very thing that guides that person into treatment. If that person is still unwilling to get help, take other steps even if it's just to gain knowledge about the illness they are suffering from. Go to groups or call help hotlines to receive further information on how you can help a loved one with a mental illness.

When someone doesn't stick to their word, let them go, they will continue to linger until you see the light for yourself. If you give someone an ultimatum and he or she chooses the best scenario that you want, and they don't live up to it, walk away. I gave an ultimatum, but when it was time for him to live up to his end, he asked for more time, and I knew right then and there, he was never going to get the help he needed. I didn't argue against the fact that he said one thing and is now doing another, all I did was present the situation in a manner that worked out in my favor. I begin to put things into perspective so that he could see I was moving in the direction that suited me best. After it was all said and done, there was nothing left for him to fight for and he had no other choice but to remove himself from the situation.

I encourage you to do the same thing, simply because someone who knows that you care about them will continue to use that emotion to adjust the playing field, so they can continue to come out on top. They are only showing you that the card that they will continue to play is the one that you make available. Once you realize that you must put your emotions to the side and focus on the mission at hand, which is getting them help, they won't have a move to make. Know that you're doing the right thing for this person by pushing them into treatment or walking right out of their life, so they can understand where your priorities are. When they comprehend what they lost in the process, it will be too late, but at least they will come to the realization of the message you were trying to send.

Chapter Seven

THE CONTAMINATION

I HAD NOT BEEN IN A relationship for a long time, so when I met this individual he seemed to be a fun filled guy who was always the life of the party. He presented himself as someone who was very giving and nurturing. Little did I know, this was the way he got into my head with every intent to manipulate me without catching on as quickly as I would have if he was straightforward with his intentions. Over time I noticed that he would never miss a chance to approach a situation that he'd benefit from. Don't get me wrong, this was also one of the things that attracted me to him because I love a go-getter. Someone with a true ambition to move forward in life is truly the type of man that I need to stand beside me to balance me out. In this situation, the type of behavior that was presented wasn't used for bettering one's stance in life, it was more or less a tactic for me to be blinded with, so he could then solidify his position in my life.

What began as hanging out as friends and talking on the phone turned into a world wind of drama. After a few drinks, he showed signs of Dr. Jekyll and Mr. Hyde; without warning, an enjoyable time could turn into a nightmare. His narcissistic traits with my strong will *not* to subject myself to anyone's foolish shenanigans made the relationship very pernicious because he wanted to have a certain type of hold over me. It never ceased to amaze me at how after a physical altercation or forcible sex, for some reason, the charm would be turned on, and I would forget everything did or said that would make me dislike the situation. As odd as that may sound, he was good with pulling the wool over my eyes long enough for him to get back into my good graces and pull a new stunt that would make me kick him out of my house.

He moved out of state and because we lived apart, he would threaten that if I did not come to visit him, an insertion of men, women, and transvestite hookers would become an issue. I never believed him until we were video chatting one night and a male friend stopped by. I can tell by the way that he was talking, that this person was coming to return a stolen item from his house. Later I found out that it was a hooker who stole his laptop and after being notified that the police were called, was returning the item for him to drop charges. Long story short, this situation brought to light that he was telling the truth and as fearful as I am, I went to go get myself tested. My results came back with a false positive, and I had to take an AIDS test every month for six months straight just to make sure.

It didn't matter if I was out and about, grabbing something to eat, or watching a movie, jealousy would come into play and unexplainable concerns would cause behaviors that I would have to endure from physical violence. What I said or did, wasn't of importance, when I stood up for myself, the physical and mental abuse began to become a daily occurrence and that's when I viewed it as a subject of violence. It got to the point where I begin to remove friends and family from my life as a safety precaution to keep them safe because of what I was experiencing.

One night after celebrating at a friend's home, we decided to keep the party going and go out to a nightclub. We picked up a friend of his along the way and stopped at his apartment, so I could change. I began to smell something funny in the air and when I went to the living room to see what it was, his friend was smoking marijuana. I asked her to stop smoking in the house and she looked at him and told him that he better check me. Of course, this rubbed me the wrong way and her and

I exchanged words. He grabbed me and push me into the bedroom and before I knew it, I was punched in the face so hard that it knocked me on the ground. I was stunned for a moment and went to the bathroom to look at my face. As soon as I saw that my lip was busted, I lost it and went into the living room to find that they were gone. I opened the front door and with a stiletto shoe in my hand, I hit him in the back of the head.

There was a scuffle to get back into the house as I was pushed into the room and began to get plummeted with fists. All the while yelling at how I embarrassed him in front of his friend and how that was his house and I had no right to tell his guest what to do. Somehow, we ended up fighting in the closet, where I tripped over my suitcase and landed backward through the clothes that were hung up. That didn't stop the punching and kicking that I endured the whole time. I couldn't see through the clothes but followed the voice spewing out threats, so I just kicked in that general direction with everything I had to give. I heard a yell and when I went to get up, the punching and stomping began all over again. I was told how bringing that pain was a big mistake and now I was about to beat within an inch of my life. Still not being able to see due to all the hung close, I put my arms up to block some of the punches, but that didn't do much, so I put both of my legs together, crunched them up to my chest, and again kicked as hard as I could. I knew I had done some damage that time because I continued to hear screams of obscenities fading away in the distance. I was unsure if I was being tricked to get me out of the closet, so I could be at a disadvantage, so I stayed there for a second and listened to see if I could hear if I was alone in the room.

Feeling a bit woozy, I managed to crawl from the closet into the bedroom and the last thing I remember is trying to stand up. When I came to, I was laying on the bedroom floor and for a second, I panicked and started looking around the room. I was alone in the bedroom and the door was closed so I went into the bathroom to look at my face. When I saw the reflection I just burst into tears because I couldn't even see my original facial structure in the reflection of the person I was looking at in the mirror.

My eyes look like something out of a horror movie because there were no whites anywhere on my eyeball because of the busted blood vessels. I had cuts on my face and it was puffy and swollen to the point where I couldn't even see my cheekbones. My arms, abdomen, behind, and legs were all sore and I could hardly move without wincing from the pain coming from these areas of my body. I took pictures of the damage with my camera phone and emailed them to my best friend. I told her if she didn't hear from me, to call the police and let them know where I was and who I was with. It was then that I heard the door; I immediately turned my phone off and hid under the bed and watched feet enter the room frantically searching for me.

The feet stopped right in front of my face and in the calmest voice I've ever heard in my life, said if I moved from under the bed I wouldn't make it through the night because there would be a round two. I can see the impression of the bed and I passed out, and when I came to once more, it was morning. I crawled from up under the bed and went to the bathroom, when I came back into the bedroom, I was too weak to do anything else, so I passed out on the bed. I woke up when I felt movement, and the first thing I heard was "Oh my God" and I was rolled over. When my face was exposed, tears begin to fall, the voice became apologetic and seemed remorseful. That was all show because in the next breath I heard, "you know I can't let you leave right?" I was supposed to fly home two days later but was made to extend my return flight for another week. I was questioned if I told anyone what happened, and I denied it. My phone was discovered under the bed and the photos I took were erased.

I was told that a run to the store would be needed for things to patch me up with and that I would be taking care of until I was able to heal and return home. After some time passed, I saw medical supplies, tons of food, and some other materials. After the food was put away, my wounds were tended to and I was told to get some rest as I watched the bedroom door close. Soon after I could hear hammering all around the house and thought it was a little odd but it all became clear once I witnessed the windows being hammered shut. In my head I was thinking, this is a bit excessive, then reality hit, and I went into panic mode because I was unsure as to what was about to take place next. I was waited on hand and foot, checked on to see if I needed anything or if I was okay. There were no obvious signs of the rage displayed the previous night. It was almost as if I were viewing a whole other entity that I was meeting for the first time who genuinely displayed compunction.

I was left alone the next day because of employment obligations and it was then that I understood the nailing of the windows shut. There was only one way in and out because the lock was broke on the sliding glass door and I didn't have the key to the deadbolt lock, which could only be unlocked from the outside. I was stuck in there without my phone or a way out. Needless to say, I made sure not to ruffle any feathers as not to wake the prodigious savage within. As the days went by my bruises began to change colors and I was able to move around a bit better. My face wasn't at its best, and I was worried that I wouldn't be able to make my flight because I didn't quite look like my driver's license photo. When I went through security, I had my shades on and the woman asked me to remove them and walk back through the metal detector, so I did, and everyone behind me gasped when they saw my face. As embarrassed as I was, they let me through and I was thankful because I was on my way home to see my kids. I had been practicing the lie that I was going to tell my family for days now, so it came out naturally when I had to explain my injuries. I said I was in a car accident, but my mother wasn't buying that because she knew better. I just didn't want my family to worry or retaliate and end up in jail over someone who clearly was not worth it.

It didn't matter how many times I tried to get away from this person, he had it dead set in his head that I was his and I belonged to him. He continued to mess up other relationships that I had to the point that I gave up dating and decided to just be alone. I didn't want to start life with someone new and subject that person to his ridiculousness. The sad part about it all was, he had already moved on to someone else, got married to this person, and had a baby on the way. What did he get out of ruining anything practical that I had in my life? I genuinely think that he just gets a kick out of being able to be a part of my life even if it represents him in a negative manner. At some point, he needs to let go, mature, and forget I even existed.

LOOKING BACK

Looking back on this situation I can honestly say that I went through the most horrifying moments of my life. I was dealing with someone who has the highest form of narcissistic personality I have ever seen in my life. There was no reasoning with him especially when it came to matters that were none of his concern. For example, when having relationships with my mother or my sons, there's no way of explaining why our relationships exist in the manner that they do because he is not a part of our family structure. It ate him up to be an outsider of our love/bonds because his jealousy would not allow him to see past anything other than hate for them because he couldn't have all of me.

On the contrary, every time he made a mistake and was about to face the consequences of said mistakes, he wanted you to take into consideration of how these consequences could affect his children. If something he did could land him in jail, he would want you to consider the fact that he would lose his job and not be able to pay child support for his kids. Therefore, pulling on your heart to make you feel sorry for the situation he put himself in with an attempt to change your mind and let him get away with whatever it was that he did, so he can stay out of jail. Any time the police were called, he made himself out to be an upstanding citizen of the community while at the same time would belittle an officer of the law if his charm didn't work on that particular policeman. If he saw that he was about to get away with the crime, he would be that officer's best friend. But if the situation wasn't going in his favor, he would criticize that officer's role, downplay any authority the officer may have, and diminish the accusation itself so it seems as if the officer is going overboard with his decision to place handcuffs on him.

Funny enough, he would never take responsibility for the things that he did or said, always making it my fault for how things worked into an argument or a physical altercation. It was my fault that people saw him as an abuser. It was my fault that people thought he used drugs. It was my fault that he cheated with women that he met for the first time. It was my fault that he started having sex with men and transvestites because I didn't come visit him enough for him to fight these urges. It was my fault that now he sees himself as a sex-addicted bisexual because that's a label I placed on him out of spite just so he can have a stigma attached to who he is as a person. Let's not forget, it was my fault that people saw him as a racist. Do I believe any of these things? Absolutely not! Simply because he was this way before he met me, I was just the only one who had enough nerve to tell him about himself when it came to these types of topics.

I can't make someone so full of hate, want nothing more in the world but to be with me, that's a crazy concept but one that he believed. In retrospect, that situation made me stronger as a person because no one else will ever get away with an ounce of the things that he did or said to me. I learned not to trust anyone who is too good to be true because there are truly people out there with personality types that build them up to seem as if they are God's gift to this world. It's hard to imagine that someone would be as egotistical as he was, conceited beyond belief when it came to knowledge, and self-absorbed to the point that his presence or even the mention of his name would bring people to rage. He let me know that it doesn't matter what position someone wants to have in your life, they will go to great lengths no matter the consequences to solidify that space.

He was always being condescending and coy with me because, in his mind, he will always be better than I am as a person. He used his addiction to drugs as a crutch to act out in a disrespectful manner by looking at other women and getting phone numbers for future use. He would talk to other women at the drop of a dime, any chance he could, whenever I was in the bathroom or if he left to get a drink. His excuse would be that he was not in his right mind, he would never do any of that to me if he were sober. Of course, I understand that all of this was because he was also a compulsive liar. What I've learned over time is, you never have to give a person a second chance if they appreciate you from the start.

He always talked about getting me pregnant, so we could have the cutest little girl ever. I know that this is only because I wanted nothing more than to have a little girl, and he played on that notion. I see that clearly now but was in a grievance toward the beginning of the situation. When things took a turn for the worst, I started to recalculate all the plans that would possibly keep him in my life for years to come. I went to the doctor and found out that I had uterine fibroids that were so overgrown that I had to get a partial hysterectomy. My doctor knew that I wanted to have a child and suggested that I have the child first because after the surgery I wouldn't be able to carry the baby myself.

After presenting this information to him he thought that it would be a great idea to postpone the surgery until after he "blessed" me with a baby girl through artificial insemination (to choose the sex of the child). His idea only fueled me with anger because he wasn't worried at all about my health but was more concerned about how he was going to be able to have a long-standing connection. There are really some people in the world who think if they share a child with you, that it is a replacement for a marriage and that's not the way they should ultimately make decisions about bringing children into the world. I, being the person that I am, decided to have the surgery as soon as possible without telling him, and I did it to avoid any unnecessary future drama. In the past, I would have sex forced on me or be so inebriated that I wouldn't put up much of a fight, and I was not about to let one of those instances be the time I would be impregnated, especially for someone else's selfish reasons.

MOVING FORWARD

IT DOESN'T MATTER how charming an individual is or how much this individual threatens you, get out of the relationship even if it means you leave with nothing. There is always a way to get out of your situation. Sometimes it may look like there's no way out and that's only because your torturer puts that idea in your head. Everyone has heard the saying that if you're constantly being told a lie, eventually you will believe it. That's true in this case also, but it's up to you to start believing in yourself and overturning all those misguided notions that an abusive boyfriend or girlfriend keeps feeding you. You must find the strength within yourself to not let someone control you mentally so that you can develop the stamina to push forward without him or her. It didn't take me long to understand that this person was not going to be a permanent figure in my life, however, I kept getting convinced that there was more to come, and I was interested in the unknown. Don't be like me, as soon as you see through someone's performance, remove yourself from the situation because it's only going to get worse.

This individual doesn't love you, because if he or she did, he or she wouldn't try to alienate you from those people in your life who care, with the intent of controlling your every move. Someone who loves you, wants to meet your friends and family, so they can be a part of your world. An individual whose sole purpose is to get you alone and ruin your relationships with others are only clearing the way for you to become solely dependent on them as a confidant, a lover, and keeper of some sorts. Take note of these types of individuals even if you aren't romantically involved, this person can be a friend or coworker. It's all about surrounding yourself with a certain type of personality that you are comfortable with, therefore the unwanted types will stick out to you and you will immediately recognize their intended motives. By practicing this type of behavior in all aspects of your life, it will make it easier for you to walk away from negative individuals without hesitating.

Your life is more important than someone else's need to control, being a punching bag isn't the image you want your kids or family to view you as because you're so much more than a victim. If you've been in an unhealthy relationship and you felt victimized, shed that stigma so you don't enter a new relationship with a lot of emotional baggage. If you do not share kids with said individual, cut off all communication, change your phone number, get a new email address, block this individual from every social media platform you are attached to. Start a new beginning, if possible, delete messages, emails, posts, burn/toss out letters and photos, and make it seem as if this person never existed.

I know you won't be able to forget things that were done or said during the situation but try your best to not let it consume you so much so that it's all you become. At one point in time in this situation, I felt as if I lost myself, and the only way I could get over that was to close myself off from everyone on the outside and regroup. The reason for this is because when you have a bad breakup, there are so many opinions that can be damaging which come from friends and family members from both sides that can make you change your mind and return to the situation you are trying to recover from. Purposely take as much time as you need until you are totally over that individual/situation and you are capable of moving forward because a new you has grown from the experience. After reorganizing your life, if anyone asks you, just politely say, "we grew apart." It's none of their business, and nine times out of 10 they just want to rehash the dreadful time in your life, so they can have something to talk about when you're not around. Don't give them the satisfaction or the ammunition to do so, because you're better than that.

Please understand that manipulators will always go for your emotions when they want to use you. They will say things like 'if you love me you'll do it' or 'you let so-and-so from your past do it, but you won't let me?' That's why it's never a good thing to tell someone's name while sharing your past experiences. It will always get tossed back in your face and leave you with regret that you shared. A lesson you can trust and the notion that you must protect yourself even against those who say they love you. They use these windows of opportunity to cut you down, so you remain controllable. Someone who manipulates will shelve your heart, so they can continue to play with your emotions. Their intentions are to get away with as much as they can before your patience runs out and they'll leave you to search for another person to fill your place. They don't truly care about the outcome because they know there will always be someone else to toy with.

Chapter Eight

NONSENSICAL

THIS PERSON CAME OFF as the strong silent type, and that's attractive because I used to like a little bit of mystery when it came to choosing a mate. Unbeknownst to me, the **silence was just a tactic** to cover up the fact that he was very negative when it came to certain topics and his behavior. He took pleasure in barking out orders (only in front of other people) to make those close to him feel insignificant, belittled, and at times obtuse. He only does this to those who he knows won't make a scene, so he comes out looking superior. And then there's the way he makes himself seem like, he puts others first because he was always going above and beyond for strangers who were in need. That's a personality trait that played in his favor because I am similar in that respect. I felt as if that was something that we had in common and could possibly grow from. As said before, I am someone who always roots for the underdog.

Unfortunately, when he helped an individual, he didn't take satisfaction from just assisting someone in need. It was something that he mentally held over their head until he needed a favor in return. For example, if he was in the neighborhood, he would bring food for anyone who was at the residence because he was coming unannounced. Then he would invite said couple out to dinner a few days later and leave them with the check to reimburse him (for his kind gesture of bringing the pizza). To me, that was very distasteful because he didn't necessarily know what their financial situation was when they came out to dinner. He also should've taken into consideration that no one asked him to stop by their residence or provide food. If the couple had anything to say about it, he would pay for his portion and go back and tell other individuals how he helped them, but when it came to reciprocate the favor, no one ever looks at all the good he's done in the past for them.

Any time a family member asked him to do something he didn't want to do, he did it with a smile on his face and then trash talked them for weeks on end. I often wondered why he didn't just say how he felt while they were in his presence, but that would mean that he had a backbone. He didn't quite know how to express himself because he would try to use big words that he didn't understand, and his delivery would get misconstrued. So, he just wouldn't say anything until he was away, and the other party was unable to defend themselves. I grew to understand the type of person he was, and it didn't sit well with me because I don't do well with negative individuals. I knew that if he was talking about his own blood-related family members in such a displeasing, insulting, and aggressive manner, that he would talk about me and my family in a worse way.

I was correct in predicting that because it came to light that he was constantly sharing private family business with outsiders. These individuals would come up and ask me about topics that were going on inside my home which had not reached the light of day because they were only discussed between he and I. It was unsettling to know that my mate was talking trash about me and my children to individuals that I didn't know or to those who I refused to associate myself with. When I would confront him about his disloyalty, he would take offense and walk away mumbling under his breath what he was too scared to say in front of my face, so we could come to a resolution. I couldn't understand why it was so important for him to have some juicy gossip to talk about that he would risk damaging his home life. It's as if the only thing he lived for is to have friends to hang around instead of having a solid family unit. It was odd to me because he stressed how significant and meaningful it was for him to have a stable relationship that he could count on.

He had the look of a person who one wouldn't want to provoke in any way, shape, or form. As time progressed, I came to find out, underneath it all, he was just a coward. He never stood up for himself when someone came to confront him about a situation. He would either threaten to call the police or simply get in his vehicle and vacate the premises. From that point on he would avoid that individual at all costs, even going as far as to change his routine. If he got backed up against the wall, he would never face the situation head-on, he would just avoid the initial issue and try to befriend the individual, so the problem would miraculously go away. That was nothing I can stand behind, especially when it came to protecting members of the household. He always wanted me to have his back, so we could provide a united front, but when an incident happened where he should've stood up for the household, he ran right over to the person and agreed that the violent attack was warranted. This is when I lost all trust and respect for who he was as an individual and as a partner.

When it came to his children, they were disrespectful, and he showed no authority, so that made me respect him less as a parent. I would tell him how I felt about how they spoke back to him, did whatever they pleased, and was disrespectful to adults in general, and he would tell me to step in and correct it because his hands were tied. I was disappointed because it's not my job to rectify his mistakes as a parent. He mostly just blamed it on their mother and did what he always did when it came to not taking responsibility, and that's ignoring the problem and sticking his head in the sand (acting like he didn't know what's going on). Toward the end of the relationship, he commended me for taking care of certain matters concerning one of his children and said that I was more of a parent to the child than his mother or himself had been up to that point.

I am my own person and I would want my significant other to be his own person. That did not happen in this case because he continuously tried to become me. Everything that I said or did, he would try to emulate or pass off as if it was his own when I wasn't around. For instance,

I would consider myself the life of the party, and someone who makes others laugh because I like to keep things light. I was always coming up with these little sayings and before long he would go around to his friends and repeat what I said as if he made it up, so he too could get the same response. Or, he would come and ask me advice about a situation that one of his friends were in and ask what I thought about the issue. I would give him my advice and the next time I would see said friend, they would rave about how he helped them through the situation because he told them to do exactly what I said, but never told them that it came from me. He would give me credit for something that someone complimented on if I was standing there, and if I was nowhere around, it was all him. But that slowly came to an end when I started to speak up and let others know that it was my work, solutions, and witty sayings. I didn't feel as if it was right that he was literally trying to take my personality to win people over just, so people would look at him in a different light.

Something that bothered me most was when he would take money from the household to give to others or showboat like he had plenty of money to give. I was baffled when I called the bank for a transaction that was unfamiliar. They gave me the information and I called only to find out that it was for a membership to a transsexual site. I confronted him, and he admitted that he was curious and had dabbled into his curiosity but had never actually had sexual contact with a transsexual. He said he had no intention of meeting anyone from the site, he just wanted to see what it was all about and that was the only way that he can have access was to sign up for a full membership. I explained to him that this put our account in the negative and he said he would cancel the membership, I informed him that I already did so, and he walked away. This was the first incident that damaged the trust.

The financial mishap did not stop there, a year later he began to have the audacity to put a strain on finances that took care of monthly bills for a hobby just to look good for his friends, family members who also participated in the hobby, and the neighborhood in general because of sponsorship. Any time there was a form of a loan that he made, he felt as if I should repay the loan because I spent most of my time in the home where the monthly bills were accumulated. What sense does that make when he resided at the residence also? If he would've let go of the hobby and his pride, there wouldn't have been a financial hole for me to dig us out of every time he wanted to prance around to attract attention. This type of behavior was very difficult for me to swallow seeing that he never wanted to progress or grow as an individual in his field. He was always comfortable with struggling and that type of lifestyle was an issue for me.

I had heard in the past that he was racist but had never seen any of it firsthand. I really began to become suspicious when he let me read a text message from his daughter and she mentioned the way her parents brought them up thinking about other races. He said he had not read that part of the text message and didn't know what she was talking about. I left it alone, but it bothered me inside because he was so quick to dismiss it and not even have a conversation to explain because she didn't know that I was going to be reading the text message. I am sure she thought it was just a private conversation that she was having with her father. One night, as he was describing an altercation with one of the members of the community (that he feared), he began describing this young man and his family with racial slurs calling them the N-word. It was then that I knew nothing was off-limits when it came to his insults and that he was probably describing me and my children in the same manner when we upset him in some way and he was venting to a listening ear. I began to cut all ties with him and walked away with my head held high.

LOOKING BACK

Looking back at this time in my life I felt as if I changed as a person into someone cold and distant to connect with. This is because when things would happen, I would shift into protector mode because I was so overwhelmed with how much drama this relationship presented me with. When I send my representative to meet someone new, I send them my best me because, at the end of the day, I'm always my best me. I'm always happy-go-lucky until someone does or says something to me in a disrespectful manner that puts them on my bad side. Being linked to this individual made me question everything that he did and said because he lied so much. It took a lot out of me to be with someone who I had to confirm with someone else if he was telling the truth or if what he told me really happen the way that he described it to me. It seemed as if there was always something going on that he never wanted to take responsibility for. His representative did not reflect any ounce of who I would be sharing my time with, so I adjusted my personality accordingly.

I wish he could've been a little more truthful about what he needed from a mate, so I can then make the choice on my own if I would be a good fit for him. The one thing that I can't stand is a compulsive liar, and he was one. It was very difficult living with this person because of his compulsion to lie at a rapid rate, these types of individuals can tell the same story and come out on the other end being the hero or the victim, depending on who he was telling the story to and how he wanted to be seen. For someone who played unintelligent to a T, he can make you feel sorry for him or envy him for his good deed or take-charge solutions. The fact that he said he wanted a family and then did everything in his power to push those close to him away was very unexpected to me. The reason why he lied so much was that he constantly needed attention, and this is common when someone has been abandoned by someone they love. This was what happened in his case, which I understand, but he shouldn't have taken it upon himself to place me in his life just to completely blindside me with his immature antics.

When I walked away from the relationship, I only felt bad for his son because I left him knowing that he had to deal with the likes of his father close to the rest of his life. With that said, I also noticed in his son, certain traits that he had adapted from his father, which is never a good thing when one damaged person is raising a child who has a chance to be his own person and not so much of a follower because this is the only thing that he knows.

If there was one thing that I could change about this person, it would be the way that he treats other individuals. I know that some people are very inconsiderate, and I only say this because not everyone is taught how to be considerate of others. This is something that my mother instilled in me at a very young age so it's second nature for me to be considerate without even thinking about it, on the other hand, it disappoints me when I cross individuals who go out of their way to be selfish especially to those individuals with whom they share a dwelling with. I've always thought it to be interesting that out in public, he would be very kind and thoughtful to strangers but when it came to his family or those who lived with him, he presented himself as self-centered, insensitive, and impolite. Therefore, it was very difficult for me to believe him when he would express how he felt about me because there is no way that someone could claim to care about me so much that they go out of their way to be oblivious to my needs, unresponsive to my concerns, and unsympathetic to emergency situations.

In the long run, I made the best choice by ending the relationship and living life alone because after he broke the trust in this situation it was all downhill from there. He continuously kept doing and saying things that would make me look at him in a questionable light. And over time I started to lose respect for him, and to be honest, I couldn't even see him as someone who had a purpose in my life. He held no merit to the decisions that I was making for my future and he made it easy for me to leave because of how much negativity he carried inside him. As soon as I left, it was like a weight was lifted off my shoulders. I could now have conversations without dumbing down my vocabulary. I didn't have to worry about someone repeating everything I said and did but twisting it to make it seem as if they were the victim, and I was free to live as I was accustomed to, no more eating chicken every day of my life simply because that was the only thing he could afford.

MOVING FORWARD

WHEN YOUR MATE must be told which conversations should be kept private and which ones are okay to share with the world, it really does damage to the trust within the relationship. When you're sharing your life with someone you should never have to filter what you say to them for fear that they might repeat your personal thoughts and concerns to other individuals. It's supposed to be a partnership between two people who have each other's backs and respect each other enough to keep the secrets of someone who confides in you. If your mate wanted their life splattered across the world for everyone to see, he or she will post on social media. When someone knows that they can trust you with their secrets, they know that they can trust you with their life.

You should find someone who values their life enough to want to make more for their efforts. Don't be with someone who's comfortable with being subpar, especially if you're someone who likes to move forward in life without being stagnant for too long. At one point he was making enough money to support everything we needed, but when he started taking money for his hobby, it put a strain on the finances, and I had to cut corners on certain things like food. That should never happen within a relationship, no one should have to eat chicken every day because it's affordable simply because their significant other wants to use the money for a hobby. Make sure that you and your mate generally have a plan of how comfortable your life should be and how you're going to reach that standard where both of you aren't struggling to live that type of lifestyle. I had never been put in a position where I had to interchange my life because of someone's amusement. I was always raised to make enough money to cover your monthly and living expenses, and whatever is left went to entertainment. If you don't have enough money to cover your living expenses, you cut out the entertainment. In his world you cut the living expenses, so he can continue to enjoy his pleasurable pastimes. Never subject yourself to the notion that this is the way to live.

I understand that there are different personality types in the world and we are bound to run across those who possess characteristics that aren't nice. But don't be with someone who belittles their loved ones (especially in front of outsiders) just to have something to talk about or prove to themselves how tough they are. The people who love us the most will always be there for us, so I find it very disturbing when other people target family members or significant others to take the blow of their insensitive behavior. Be with someone who has the confidence to stand on their own without tearing others down. I tend to look at these individuals as weak and unable to communicate well because they must hide behind a tough guy/girl persona. Invest in someone who's going to focus on you and the relationship without having to show off in this manner. Not only is it tacky, but it speaks volumes about this person's character and might be the first hint that this person is not for you. Eventually, these people may show qualities of negative behaviors, lack of social skills, and violence.

When you're dating someone, in the beginning, make sure that the representative reflects the person they are representing. I don't know how to stress this enough, because this is where most of us go wrong when choosing to stay with an individual who we thought we were getting in the beginning. Everyone will always put their best foot forward, that's a given. When you are in search of a serious long-term relationship, spend some time with this individual alone and in a public setting. The best way to get to know someone for who they truly are is to be taken around their friends and family. If that person acts the same around people who know him or her best, nine times out of 10 you're getting a genuine feel for who this person is.

I must be blunt when I say, dumb can change a man/lady. Don't let someone else's uneducated mind, make you lose your educational value. When someone can't quite communicate how they are feeling, what they mean, or the point that they are trying to make due to their limited vocabulary, it will cause problems within the relationship. When having conversations or even arguments, the point would be lost because I would be trying to figure out the words he meant to say compared to the words that came out of his mouth during his thought process at the time.

When I would stop and ask him if he meant something else, he would lose his train of thought as would I, and then the topic of conversation switched to what he should have said. I'm not saying that you must be on the same educational level as your mate, because this may be something that doesn't bother you. As for me, I could never have a relationship with someone who's not on my same educational level. Find what suits you best and if it works for you, move forward with grace.

At the end of the day, if you don't respect someone as a person, you never value the role they play in your life. It doesn't matter what they say or do, it won't count for anything because you see this person as subpar. When you've mastered valuing yourself, you learn to value your partner for the substance they also bring into the relationship.

Chapter Nine

THE CHEATING

THERE HAVE BEEN MEN in my life who cheated on me and as a young person, I would think that it was because I didn't have what the other person had. I wasn't tall enough, I didn't have the body that she had, or I didn't look like she looked. As an adult, I know it doesn't matter who I am or what I did or didn't do, these individuals were going to cheat anyway because of their own insecurities. Not knowing that at the time, I felt like it was my fault that I wasn't doing something to fulfill my half of the relationship, so this individual had to seek what he needed elsewhere. It's not my fault at all, because we all make decisions according to our morals and morally I am not the type of person to condone cheating just because I feel as if someone failed me in a relationship.

If my needs are not being met mentally or physically in a relationship, that means that there is some type of communication failure and I need to address the issue with my mate in hopes of rectifying the problem, so we can advance the relationship. Once we are both aware of the situation and understand what must be done, we will make a solid attempt to try to recover and get things back on track. I have done this over the years and for someone who wants to be in the relationship, he has worked with me to make sure we are both progressing. For someone who continues to cheat regardless of the meetings of the mind or past conversations to improve the relationship, this person is clearly letting me know that he is not ready to be in a relationship with me. He was not willing to invest in the time that we needed, therefore he would never be able to love me the way I need him to as a partner. Anyone who didn't put in the work to make the relationship perform in a manner that it needed to, isn't the person who was willing to make sacrifices for my love to last and was a clear sign for me to walk away.

Cheaters have no business being in a relationship because they don't change their ways because of the person, they stop sleeping around when they get tired of that life. They may even give up that type of behavior when they find someone who's worthy of not losing. They may have an epiphany along the way and realize how painful it was for them to use other individuals for their personal gain or pleasure when they think of how they cheated on past mates. Most of the time this epiphany occurs after someone they really gave their all to cheats on them. It's funny how clear someone's perspective can be when the shoe is on the other foot and they are not on the winning team of those insensitive, distressful, and malicious results. It's best for cheaters to recognize that they don't want to be in a committed relationship and that they should continue being single. The honest thing for a cheater to do is to be forthright and tell the interested party that they are not seeking anything permanent. This way the person knows up front who they are dealing with and can make the decision on their own whether they want to subject themselves to getting involved with someone of this nature.

From my personal experience with someone who has cheated in every relationship he has had, it was because he had abandonment issues, so he never wanted to be alone. For him, anyone would do as long as he didn't sleep alone at night. Over the years he developed a sexual addiction and not knowing how to control his urges, he had no intentions of being faithful to anyone that entered his life. It was a plus that he had a relationship and even preferred it because he could go cheat and would always have someone to come home to. Even though he had a family, he still struggled with sexual addiction and it ultimately ruined his life because he lost everything due to his constant cheating. Lo and behold I came along and filled a void of having the much-needed partner, yet he continued to cheat to fulfill his sexual desires. The relationship wasn't worth saving because the addiction was far too rampant, and I wasn't willing to continue to put myself at risk for STDs simply because he had no regard for the outcome of his actions. He enjoyed living that type of life and I valued my life more than the relationship, so I was happy to exit with my head held high.

LOOKING BACK

BEING ON THE other end of someone's cheating ways can take a toll on you as an individual. I know this to be true because I have stepped out of my character due to a fit of rage when finding out that someone was disloyal to me. I am not proud of my behavior, but at the time I was young and foolish to believe that my devotion to certain individuals would be enough to keep them faithful. It wasn't my fault that they cheated, they needed a way out and some people cheat for that very reason. Others cheat because they want to have their cake and eat it too, they're just selfish that way. Women don't always start out scorn, there are usually some incidents that take place to form her into a person who doesn't trust easily.

I was with an individual who not only cheated with people that I didn't know, he chose to cheat on me with those who knew me and was close enough for me to have in my home. When these things came to light I was very livid, to say the least, and my reaction at the time was raw and impulsive. I am in no way proud of the behavior I displayed at the time, as I have now learned how to control my temper as an adult when facing situations that may lead me to a life behind bars. It's amazing how one's emotions can take over their whole thought process as they lose control and is taken over by extreme anger. I am, of course, describing myself because I was filled with so much fury at the fact that two people who knew me, had met extended family members, and who I trusted with my children, committed such a distasteful act against me as a person.

There is one moment that I am very ashamed of, this happened as a result of someone cheating on me with a person I knew. I was at home sick and this individual wanted to go out to a nightclub. After getting into an argument he went without me, which was fine because I just planned on sleeping for the rest of the night. I was getting phone calls from friends asking why I wasn't at the club and I should head that way because they were having an overwhelming amount of fun. I caved in and thought I should go dance and sweat out the sickness, plus I could sleep the following day. I got dressed thinking that I would surprise my mate and true enough when I got there it was packed, and I was ready to have some fun. When the bartender saw me (who was a friend of mine), she told me after I walked around to come see her because she had something to tell me. I walked around and didn't see my mate anywhere in sight, I said hello to a few friends and when I went to go get a drink the bartender told me that she saw my mate and his best friend leave with my old babysitter and her best friend.

Here is where I started to go insane! I didn't know where this girl lived, and I didn't want to go to his best friend's house because he was married with two kids and one on the way. The only thing left for me to do was to go to my house and prepare for the long night that was ahead of me. Seeing that I was the only breadwinner, I took everything that I ever bought him and confiscated it. In my head I was thinking, how could I be so foolish as to buy you the finer things in life, only so you can go out and sleep with other women who are attracted to you now that I've upgraded your status? I ransacked my closet and everything he came into the relationship with went into a suitcase that I set outside the front door. All the items I bought him went into a few large storage bins. I placed them at the front of the door so when he came in all he had to do was take them outside. Mind you, I poured hot sauce and bleach on everything before I sealed them up.

For some reason, that wasn't good enough for me, so I packed up every video game/console and put them in the attic. I knew that he would be angry once he saw what I did to his clothes and that this would obviously be the beginning of a physical altercation, so to make the odds even (because he was bigger than me), I put canned vegetables in the cushions of the sofa so that I would have one at arm's reach at all times. Now keep in mind that this is me purely working off rage and I'm just trying to cover every possible scenario that I have running around in my head of how this is going to end. I changed my clothes because I'm ready for war and I put my hair up because I don't want him to have any type of advantage. Then I wait, I wait some more, and I end up going to bed because it's getting late and I figure he must be spending the night where he's at.

I heard the car door and jumped right back into my war clothes because there was no way I was going to wait until the morning to confront him. He came into the room and was surprised that I was up, he asked me why all his stuff was packed up and why wasn't I in bed because I was sick. I quickly bypassed that because he didn't have any authority to be asking me questions at this point. I asked him where he was at because I went to the club and was told that he left with so-and-so. He said it wasn't what I thought and if I didn't believe him, he could take me to where he just came from and they will tell me themselves. I smiled, grabbed my keys, and headed for the car. He gave me directions to the place as I was driving, all the while saying that they might be sleep because it's late. We pulled up to the apartment and I got out, so he followed suit. I told him to take me to the apartment and when we got there, I put him in front of the door and I moved out of sight.

She opened the door naked and asked if he forgot anything. I pushed him into the apartment and punched her in the face, that's when we fell to the floor because we tripped over his and her best friends who were naked in a sheet. I kept unleashing my anger on her while her friend was yelling in the background and the two guys pulled us apart. I punched my mate in the face, so he could let me go and I walked out of the apartment to my car. I backed out of the parking space and he jumped in front of the car, I pushed forward as he bounced off the hood and rolled onto the ground. My first thought was, I can't *believe* I just hit him. When I stopped at the stop sign, I looked in my rearview just in time to see him standing up. My second thought was, he's okay, I'm not going to jail. Everything happened so fast and it clearly snapped me back to reality because I didn't even know that I was capable of behaving in such a manner.

He ran over to the car, knocked on the window, and pleaded for me to let him in because he was sorry and didn't mean to hurt me. I unlocked the door and as we traveled back in silence, I couldn't even look in his general direction. When we returned, he tried to follow me to the bedroom, I announced that he was going to be sleeping on the couch. How could he ever think he could go off and have relations with someone else and then come sleep in my bed? Really? The next morning, I got up and took a hot shower because, for me, it was a new day. I went to the kitchen and started cooking breakfast, he got up to take a shower and then realized that he didn't have any clothes in the closet. I told him I put his close in those bins by the door and when he opened it he smelled the hot sauce. He said he guess he deserved that and he would start washing them after he ate. I said there was no need to wash them because they were also bleached and that he will be leaving today with what he came into the relationship with and that was the items that were in the suitcase. He said he didn't have anywhere to go, so I coldly informed him that he had a place last night and he can return to that spot without any communication from me further. I took the keys to my car and my house as he picked up his suitcase and headed out the door.

As I said before, this was not my proudest moment in life, but it took someone pushing me that far to know that even *I* could lose control. Because I know that I am capable of acting in such a way that may cause me to lose everything that I've ever worked for, I make it a point to think things through before I act on how someone else has handled me. That is the best advice that I can give someone who has been cheated on, although it is difficult, retaliation can lead you to a place where you will be paying for that mistake for years to come. I am thankful that I did not harm him in a way that he could not recover from. I am glad that I was able to learn from this huge mistake so that I do not repeat this type of behavior moving forward. Now, as an adult, I am efficient enough (because of experience) to control my anger when I have been emotionally dragged through the mud. It's better for me to voice what I'd like to do than to act on it.

MOVING FORWARD

Moving forward from these experiences, I've learned to ask questions before getting involved with someone, just so I can get a better understanding of who they are as a person. I used to believe that everyone has a past, and I can only judge that person from the experience that I share with them from the day we are committed moving forward. I can't believe I used to live that way, now I want to know about their past because it gives me a better sense of why their relationships didn't work out. If they are unable to have successful past relationships that held some type of substance, generally this person is not for me. If they were the common denominator of why the relationships ended, that is a big red flag for me and that's my cue to leave that for someone who is willing to take on that type of challenge. My number one question to ask is if they have ever been cheated on or have cheated in past relationships. If they have been cheated on they are less likely to cheat because they know how it feels to be betrayed. If they admit to cheating on a past mate, I want to know why and how it all played out, so I can make the best decision for myself.

If you are in a relationship and there is someone else that you are interested in and feel as if you need to pursue this person, it's only right that you leave your current situation. This will prevent your partner from having to suffer through doubting who they are as a person because your actions have developed insecurities in your mate, especially if you give them no reason whatsoever behind your behavior. It's a very simple step to take, leave the relationship before you do something foolish. You never know if they may temporarily go insane and end up physically hurting you. There is a reason why there is a crime of passion law because people temporarily lose their minds and do things that they wouldn't ordinarily do if they were thinking straight. It's not morally right to put someone in a position where they may be on trial for their life because you couldn't control your urge to cheat. The aftermath of being cheated on could scar someone emotionally for the rest of their lives and possibly destroy any future relationships that they may have. I believe that that's enough for someone to have to bear without causing further damage.

For those who have been cheated on, I'm pretty sure some of the things that I have said have hit home for you. I hope you are now in a place to understand that someone else's psychological adventure has nothing to do with you personally. You are merely a pawn in this person's life. It is time for you to take your power back and no longer take on the responsibility for a cheating mate's actions, dealings, or lifestyle. You must believe that you only allow things that you tolerate, I say this because when you get enough of someone cheating on you, you'll wake up and understand that you deserve better. You must be strong enough to know your value because it sets the standard for your self-worth. If you believe that you did something wrong to deserve being cheated on or misused, you're wrong. The person that cheats depends on the fact that you think you're worthless. This way he or she can continue to cheat because he or she knows that you don't value yourself enough to let him or her go. It doesn't matter how much you love this person or how much they've done for you, if you are in a monogamous relationship and your significant other cheats on you, leave. Sure, it will sting for the moment, but what you do is take away that person's power to continue to hurt you by cheating again. I will say it once more, leave. It's that simple and you will save yourself from having to suffer through that same hurt repeatedly.

Chapter Ten

THE PHYSICAL ABUSE

I ENDURED QUITE A BIT OF physical and mental abuse from individuals who I thought cared for me and my well- being. That was not the case and many of these past situations failed because said individuals did not want to see me grow into someone with confidence, independence, and positiveness. Although I possessed these things, they were a threat to the other party's ego or manhood. Whether physical or mental, abuse is harmful and because I *thought* I was in love at times, I followed the example that was given to me as a young child. I fought for relationships that were built on my failure as a strong-willed person who was dead set on succeeding. Not knowing at the time that my self-worth was truly valued in dignity and quality of life; I continued to subject myself to such behavior from those who thought very little of themselves because of how substantial I felt about myself.

It always starts out as mental abuse, I'm guessing because it's a way of testing the waters so to speak. If an individual was able to get in my head about something personal that happened to him, I felt I had to be more willing to stay and not walk out of that person's life. This was a fault of my own because that type of tactic is commonly used to gain sympathy for the abuser. When someone would tell me that no matter what, people constantly walked out of their lives, I made it my mission to be the person who stayed regardless of what the conditions were because I felt bad that those before me made him feel unwanted. For some reason, I had it in my head that I could change his perception and in turn, he could develop a sense of self and not feel worthless anymore. I didn't understand at the time that that was not my job nor my place to step in and build up an individual who didn't show me the same respect. As a person, that's who I was without comprehending that there are some individuals out there who feed off good intentions.

Now that said individual had my mental state right where he felt comfortable, he decides to up the ante by introducing physical abuse into his plan. A slap every so often wasn't bad, it really didn't hurt that much, I can take it because it was something that I said, and maybe I even deserved it because I pushed the conversation too far. That was my mindset years ago as I tried to make excuses for someone treating me in this manner. I couldn't say that I didn't know better because all along I knew the right thing for me to do was to walk away and not set a bad example for my children to witness. By staying in such a situation, the only thing I did was convinced myself that I was strong enough to take whatever came my way because in the end, I was helping someone find himself. That statement couldn't have been more wrong, the person already knew who he was from the beginning, I was the one with the clouded mindset.

Before long, I've figuratively given this person a free pass to mentally and physically abuse me as much and as often as he felt free to because I never left. Over time I would fight back to show that he didn't totally break me, and I still have the will to stand up for myself when I've deemed enough is enough. This type of behavior only put me on the same level as he was and at that moment, he wins because that was his goal from the beginning. To totally pull me out of my character and to make me into the monster that he clearly he knew he was from the start. I was no longer positive toward this individual because I knew he was full of nothing but toxic outcomes. Why am I having full-on fistfights with someone who claims he cares about my well- being? Why are their arguments over things that are so small that they could have been dismissed in seconds, yet turn into physical altercations that last into the wee hours of the night? How was it possible for this individual to bring out such hatred, a desire to harm, and mental ability to wish death in such torturous ways from me? This is not the person that I was before he came along. Nor is it the person that I want my children to view or categorize me as when they look back and envision me in their childhood.

LOOKING BACK

When close friends used to ask me why I don't just leave, I gave the typical response of, "because I love him." This is something that I had been hearing all my life from multiple men and women who were in similar situations. That statement should no longer be the norm when discussing why one doesn't find it necessary to preserve his or her life. I know now that these people were toying with my emotions because they have insecurities within themselves that they aren't willing to face and would rather take out on those around them. To them, it's everyone else's fault why they behave, think, and react the way that they do. Clearly, in retrospect, that is not the case and it is *my* responsibility as someone who is in control of the outcome of my own life to correct this notion. I am not someone's personal punching bag because he couldn't handle the downfalls in his life. I must stand up for myself as an individual who comprehends that this type of behavior is unacceptable.

I had to change who I was as a person in order to break the cycle when not putting myself in these types of situations. I no longer surround myself with negative or narcissistic beings simply because I know better than to get into a battle of wits with an unstable mind, which may lead to physical altercations. I gracefully remove myself from the circumstances or person because I do not wish to invest energy into a lose-lose situation by entertaining the notion that this person is going to snap into reality and gain a sense of respect out of one conversation. It took me a while to develop this type of zero-tolerance against mental and physical abuse, but that all stems back to knowing and understanding my self-worth as an individual. Once I gained a clear perceptive of how important my self-worth was to me, it began to change my life and in turn changed who I allowed to enter and stay in my personal space. At this point in time, it's difficult for me to associate myself with those who notice my self-worth and choose to disrespect it.

Therefore, they make it easier for me to walk away without feeling any guilt for not assisting them with finding a more positive side of themselves. As I mentioned before, it's not my place to want to change someone into a positive source of energy. These abusive people knew their objectives when they picked me out of a crowd and placed themselves into my life. Turning on the charm, in the beginning, was just a way for them to create a delusional bond so I could become attached to the person they felt I would empathize with for their unfortunate upbringing. When their true colors come out, I have no sympathy for their past misery because they used their misfortune to create disappointment, shame, and regret when it came to my emotions. I was disappointed in the fact that I couldn't see them for who they really were, I hid in shame because of the bruises that were all over my body, and I regretted the fact that I lied and created cover stories, so friends and family wouldn't retaliate in my defense.

I can now spot these types of people from a distance and choose to stay clear of their path of unnecessary drama because I pity them. They exert so much energy into tearing another person down that they can't even take the time to invest in themselves. It is clear that they lack guidance and don't possess the ability to allow someone to get close enough to help them out of the black cloud they choose to live in. It's unfortunate that they would rather wreak havoc on those who are willing to give their all just, so they can have a better outcome in life. It makes me upset when I see a friend who is dealing with the likes of a narcissistic soul because I know the solution is to walk away. If you don't grant others the right to abuse you from the start because you know you deserve better, it becomes easier to create distance from those types as you move throughout life.

MOVING FORWARD

IT'S INSANE HOW someone can be attracted to you because you are full of such light, and then try to do everything in their power to snuff out every existence of said light just so they can keep you in the dark. It's sad when you must be aware of people who wish to harm your mental and physical state. I've seen it repeatedly in friends' relationships who asked me for advice on what they should do after explaining their situation. I'll tell you what I tell them, now is the time to quickly develop a sense of self-worth and acquire a taste for having a zero tolerance for physical and mental abuse. Why continue to put yourself in harm's way for someone who cares nothing about you? Just because you are going through a difficult time in life at this point, doesn't mean that there isn't someone out there who would treat you better than you treat yourself.

That should be your standard, only be with someone who treats you better than you treat yourself. You don't punch yourself in the face, you don't tell yourself how worthless you are, you don't find pleasure in putting people down just to lift yourself up daily. If you don't treat yourself horribly, why would you allow someone else to come into your life and form you into a miserable, depressed, tormented, heartbroken, injured, and shameful person? When you're in a relationship with someone who builds you up as an individual, you should remain mentally and physically healthy throughout your courtship before you even think of marrying said person. If you have experienced something that has ultimately strained the relationship, marrying this person is not going to improve, revamp, or rectify any current or past negative issues. It's time to walk away.

There is never an excuse to not leave or simply act like you don't know better. I love him or her, is no longer an acceptable statement as to why you choose to give up on life. You can't love someone who doesn't love you enough to respect you as a person or significant other. Anyone who takes advantage of the fact that you are sharing your life with him/her says loudly through their actions that they don't value you. They take that opportunity and use it to gain the upper hand. Physical and mental abuse comes from the other person's insecurities and should never be disguised as love. If you are in this type of situation, know that you are the only one who can change or stop the circumstances that you're in, because the other person in your life who subjects you to this type of behavior feeds off the negativity.

He or she will never wake up one morning out of the blue, come to his or her senses, and seriously approach you with the statement of, "I am genuinely sorry for everything I put you through. I value you as a person, and because of that thought alone, I am walking out of your life, so you can once again find peace and happiness with someone who loves and respects you." An abuser would never take your feelings into consideration above his or her own simply because that would make him or her human and he or she is incapable of acting in such a thoughtful manner. You may receive a statement similar to the above after something tragic has happened to the individual or he or she (by some miracle) attends many therapy sessions.

Please know that your life is one that is worth living without being tormented along the way. You were not placed on earth to become another individual's whipping boy simply because this is their sport of choice. Find it within yourself to muster up the strength to walk out the door, even if it's with nothing but the clothes on your back and if you have them, the children in your arms. Nothing else matters but your life! You can get another place to live, you can purchase more clothes at a later date, you can replace anything else that you left behind apart from your life. The more you stay in an abusive relationship, the more you risk the days you have left on this earth. You really must look at it from that aspect because your abuser is continuously getting comfortable with the fact that you're going to cover for him or her and they will get away with it because there is no record of abuse. Pick up the phone and call 911 every single time! Don't have someone call on your behalf, because in some states that doesn't count as you personally reporting it. Even if you must wait until you are out alone, go to the police station and make a report, but put it on record. Preserve your right to live.

Once you escape from an abusive/toxic person, make sure to keep a record of stalking. Save texts, emails, and phone messages to prove threats or non-wanted communication. Send a clear message saying you no longer want to be contacted by all or any social media resources, phone communication of any kind, email, texts, snail mail, or you will report him or her to the local authorities! Keep your word to preserve your life! With the proof of harassment built up, you can go to court and get a restraining order. Continue to keep a record even after the order is in place so you can report it and be able to file charges! Never let him or her back in your life after that point, once you do, all that work you did to protect yourself will be voided. And the restraining order won't hold weight because you went against it by allowing him or her to enter your life again.

BROKEN PROMISES

March 19, 7:30pm - The first time I was hit because of something I said. Blood filled my mouth and embarrassment set across my face.

March 22, 1:49pm - My mouth was still bruised from the backhand I received, brought on by a lost temper and I was then beaten with a belt. I was promised it wouldn't happen again, as I was given reassurance that it all happened due to stress.

April 19, 2:58am - Busted blood vessels in my eyes make it hard to see my eye color (it took over a year for my nerves to reconnect).

April 19, 9:12am - The aftermath of the night before. I was promised if I didn't report the damage that it would never happen again. Nothing but lies!

April 20, 2:50pm - I was still in disbelief every time I looked in the mirror. How could I have allowed this person to slip through the cracks?

April 24, 5:12pm - The swelling has gone down, but I'm beyond broken. My heart is barely holding on to hope and I'm ready to give up on understanding love.

April 25, 10:19am - The bruises are black and blue, but it's getting better.

April 25, 7:39pm - The whites in my eyes are coming back and I don't look too bad with makeup covering my eyes and face. This nightmare was almost over.

May 10, 9:15am - So much for promising to keep ones word. It shows how someone can plead with you for forgiveness and recant their words for their own selfish gain.

July 22, 9:17pm - Not much to physically see, the pain within my burning lips were enough to record this small upset.

August 14, 7:12pm - Another drunken night when Mr. Hide came out to shatter my pride. God forbid I stand up for what I believe in.

August 18, 6:10pm – Beaten with a fire poker. Promises lost in the wind.

August 19, 11:46am - Recovering again, and yes; you guessed it, the other party was sorry and regretful. I on the other hand, I was full of rage.

September 9, 9:56pm - A night of tussling because someone looked at me? How was that my fault?

September 10, 9:34pm - Days like this never get better, the gifts don't mean anything, and I wish I had someone who knew how to love me. Just my personal thoughts.

October 9, 12:39am - A few punches wrapped with a belt buckle. It was over quick, but I made up my mind. I was done with protecting other people, I was making a report of this to the local authorities. I vowed to never take any type of abuse from that point on.

I Started To Become Mentally Stronger Than My Abuser. Once I Accomplished This, It Was Easier To Walk Away!

Chapter Eleven

THE SEXUAL ABUSE

AS A YOUNG CHILD, MY WHOLE view on life was changed over a summer by a predator. He was supposed to be someone that I was able to trust and turned out to be a wolf in sheep's clothing. The molestation started in first grade and didn't end for years. I was threatened that if I ever told anyone that he would kill my mother and brothers. I was also told that every time there was any resistance on my part, that my mother would be the one to receive my punishment in the form of a beating. Not knowing at a young age what manipulation was all about, I felt trapped, alone, and disgusting all at the same time. Clearly, the beatings he gave my mother on a consistent basis weren't because of something that I did, but because of his alcoholic rages. Nevertheless, I associated those beatings with the molestation and blamed myself for my mother's pain.

As I got older, I began to understand that what was going on was not my fault and that it was wrong. It was up to me to stop this individual from taking control over my life, so I began to sleep with knives under my pillow just so I could feel safe. I spent as little as time possible at home when he was there and when I did come home, I would go straight to my room. I made sure that the lock on my bedroom door was locked all the time, so if he made a move, there would be some indication or noise that would get the attention of others. After he was removed from the household, I was sure that that was the end of my experience with sexual abuse. I was wrong.

There was an incident that happened on my 16th birthday. I stayed up all night the night before waiting until midnight, so I can begin to celebrate my sweet 16. After school, I had a dentist appointment for a routine cleaning and I was excited about getting home so I can celebrate my birthday. I was passing my mother's office and decide to stop and see if she would give me a ride. She wasn't there and after waiting for her over an hour, one of her soldiers offered me a ride home. I had seen him there before and he came to our house a few times, so I felt as if he was trustworthy. When we were leaving the post, he turned the wrong way and said he had to go to his house to grab something real quick and then he would drop me off. Once we arrived at his apartment, he asked me to come in because it was going to take him a minute or two to find what he was looking for. I came in, sat on the couch, and after a few minutes of rambling in his room he came out and sat next to me. He began to ask me personal questions that were a bit intrusive, it was putting me in an uncomfortable state, it was at that point that I got up and tried to leave. He served three years in prison for that attack.

My life was forever changed at that point. Something was taken from me and it was more than my pride. I stopped wearing skirts or dresses because if someone was going to rape me, I didn't want them to have easy access. In my mind, if I wore pants I would have more time to fight or draw attention to what was going on. To this day I only wear skirts when I am out with my husband and they usually go all the way to the ground. I stopped hanging out with all my friends and became a homebody because I never wanted to put myself in the position where someone would see me out and about and would want to harm me. I lost a great majority of my male friends because some of their parents caught wind of what happened to me and felt as if I were damaged goods. I could only guess that they presumably thought any male I associated with would be in harm's way of being accused as a rapist. I stopped celebrating my birthday at that instant because it was no longer a day of festivity. I started acknowledging my birthday again when I was 22 and would never go out to commemorate the occasion. Today, I spent a significant amount of time with my husband on that day to create positive memories.

I never thought that I would have to protect myself against someone that I was dating when it came to rape. Unfortunately, I'm not the only one who has experienced this type of blindsided confusion. It's one thing to be raped by a stranger, and it's a totally different stupefaction to experience this bewilderment from someone I knew and was in a relationship with. There are so many things that were running through my mind because this is the person who is supposed to protect me from outsiders. How could this be happening to me when the other party knew a bit of my past with sexual abuse? How could a mate be someone who slipped under the radar? How could he pose as someone who cared about me when he knew he was capable of tearing my life apart with this sexual act? That was it, I made up my mind. No man could ever be trusted no matter who he says he is or what he stands for. I would spend the rest of my life being on guard and not being able to fully trust any man that came along simply because I don't know his intentions. I remain guarded to this day… I trust no one.

LOOKING BACK

THE SEXUAL MOLESTATION that happened to me as a young child could have absolutely been avoided. This person's family knew that he molested his niece and failed to tell my mother about his past because they believed him when he said he was cured. They wanted to give him a fresh start in life because he started going to church and memorized the Bible. The truth is, there are many people who know the Bible, yet the only other entity that knows the Bible as well as God is the devil. Looking back on that whole situation, in my eyes, his family is just as guilty for what happened to me. If these people would have warned my mother about who he really was and the things that he did to his own family member, my mother would have the necessary information needed to make the choice to not marry a child molester.

I find it very puzzling that no one thought to mention what he did to his own niece until after my mother confronted them about what he had done to me. I took that abuse for years and even in that experience I begin to fight back. I became hollow, numb, and turned off to men of color and even men in general because every time I had a sexual experience it would take me back to that place. Not wanting to bring up the past abuse, I became attracted to those of another race and women. Not to mention, I would not let my children sleep over at their friend's houses when they were young because of the molestation. This is because I had a friend spend the night as a child and that person tried to molest her also.

Being raped by individuals who knew me affected my future relationships so much so that I became an extremely private person. I don't let people in easily, and it's hard for me to trust people because I always have my guard up. These types of individuals earned my trust and I put my wall down long enough for them to be comfortable with the fact that they could make a heinous move. I'm not going to say I set myself up to fail because I truly didn't see any red flags or signs of violent lust in these individuals. After these incidents happened and I lived alone, I would never meet a male friend in my home and I always had a friend or family member come visit me when there was a male servicing something in my dwelling. When I use to go out with female friends, I would always be in fight mode when we went out to public places and I made sure to be aware of my surroundings. The aftermath of these perplexed experiences made me conscious of those who hide in plain sight.

I accept who I am because I understand that I could have totally become someone else if none of this ever happened to me. I'd like to think that I have grown from these experiences and turned them into lessons learned. I'm not saying that the things I did to rebuild myself were perfect, but I am saying that I am no longer blinded to the fact that horrible things happen daily and sometimes those appalling things are done by people we trust. I had to explain to my two sons when they got older why I never allowed them to spend the night at other people's homes if there was a male in the house. It was difficult, but it was something I felt they should know. When they were young they didn't know that I was ultimately trying to protect them, and I didn't feel as if they would understand until they reached a certain age. Everything else that I have changed in my life is to simply adapt in the event that something may occur. Sexual abuse and rape, change not only the body but the mindset of an individual who experiences it, and I am no exception to the rule. I am merely here to speak my truth in hopes that someone else can avoid causing themselves more harm by staying in their current situation. The best thing I ever did in these situations was when I mustered up the courage/strength to report them and walk away.

MOVING FORWARD

I MAKE IT a point not to ever vouch for an individual because I don't know who they are or what they are capable of. I don't want to be responsible for another person gaining trust in the Wolf in sheep's clothing by confirming that he or she is genuinely an honorable member of society. We never really know who we're dealing with until after the fact. For example, there are many stories about people who have done horrific things and when the news reporter interviews the neighbor he or she says, "he was always nice, helped us with the yard, and always donated." They always seem to be so shocked. It's the same way when a current mate experiences physical or sexual abuse and the ex-mate of the abuser stands there in denial because they never encountered episodes of this nature with *that* particular person. Please don't speak up for a person if you are unaware of that person's current mental state. This is not to say that you shouldn't stick up for family members whom you know for fact is not a sexual abuser. Just know that there are abusers who depend on those who are going to reaffirm their position as Wolf in order to continue to get away with heinous acts.

I personally feel that it is up to the victims to report these types of individuals. If the victims of the men who abused me actually reported them, I would have been spared the agony of experiencing such horrific ordeals in my life. It's ultimately up to us to break the cycle of protecting these abusers, even if they are members of our family. Victims should never feel victimized by the public, society, or friends and family. As long as we continue to practice silence, we put others at risk who will wonder the same thing that I did as I got older. Why didn't anyone speak up? If this person had a history of abuse, why is the family keeping it a secret? I was sexually abused, and I felt tainted by the act itself, infected by guilt, and contaminated by public scrutiny. It wasn't until later that I'd come to understand that talking about it took away the power of the abuser. I'm going to continue to talk about it because I want others to be protected from corrupt individuals.

Abusers will continue to get away with what they've done because victims choose to hold it all in and never speak of it again. It's not your fault that someone else finds it difficult to cope with life so he or she decides to torment another soul. Just because you got rid of that person and that person is no longer in your life doesn't mean that that's where it all stops. This may be where it stopped for you at the moment, but it is still your responsibility after you put yourself back together, to expose this person because no one else is stopping him or her from terrorizing other people. If that was the case, they would've been stopped after the first attempt, put in jail or punished, and then had no other victims. This is me standing up for myself in hopes that I can save someone else from experiencing the vile and shameful things that I went through in life. None of these people were able to break me to the point that I wanted to take my own life and I look at that as an achievement. I was strong enough to build myself back up and go on living in a positive and happy manner.

There is always life after dark times so never give up on yourself because suicide is not an option that fixes everything. It makes things worse for those you leave behind. It was up to me to set an example for my children that they can always choose to make life better just by walking away from a situation, learning from that experience, and tweaking their life so they can grow as an individual with the intent of avoiding the same mistakes. You can reinvent yourself into a whole new person and start a fresh life. Moving forward is the key to survival. If you let what an abuser did to you affect you for the rest of your life to the point where you suffer from depression or you're only interested in those who continue to abuse you because this is all you know, you will always have a difficult road ahead. The hardest part is finding the courage to leave. You must mentally prepare yourself for the challenging time of picking yourself back up.

This means you are going to have to tell your story to a friend, family member, or professional with the intention of receiving support. I promise you, every time you explain your situation and the events leading up to that point, it'll get easier. And because now you're on the outside of everything you went through, you'll be able to see the situation for what it was and that alone will make it simpler to deal with. The aftermath won't be so bad because you've already lived through the most horrific part of your life. You will have a clear-cut view of who this person really is because he or she is no longer in control over your mental state. It will become evident that this person means you harm because his or her intentions are now translucent. It is up to you to get over this hurdle and find the ability to keep moving forward.

Chapter Twelve

THIS IS MY BEGINNING

THIS IS THE FIRST TIME IN my life that I have ever experienced being in love because he knows how to love me. That statement alone is so powerful because it is mindful and full of clarity. It doesn't even feel cliché to say that he is the one I've been searching for all my life, because he is the personification of what I always thought my ideal mate should be. He is truly a man's man in the way that he loves me unconditionally. He is supportive of my goals and dreams as he puts me first and helps me understand his world. Although at times his world is quite different from mine, we share way too many things in common to allow that to ever become an issue.

When we first met, we ascertained just how much in common we had by the lifestyles we led. We shopped at the same places and have similar tastes which meant that once we moved in together, we realized we have just about two of everything. It was becoming a little weird that we had the same kitchen gadgets, bedding, workout stats, and vehicles of the same color. The love we share for food is exciting, we both are great chefs in the kitchen and because we are competitive, we often have cookoffs to see whose dishes are better. Our passion for music is moving, he plays multiple instruments (and is currently teaching me the drums), while I love to sing and dance. We raised our children differently, but we do our best to make sure they turn out right, while at the same time incorporating what we learn from each other, because as he says, "we're in the business of making men and women."

With that said, we make sure we model our relationship after something the children want from their future mates. They have already seen what a toxic relationship looks like because of our past relationships, so it was very important for us to set the tone to what a positive correlation can be when you find the right person. We take the time and effort to address situations immediately, honestly, and maturely. This is the only way that we ultimately respect one another's assessment of a certain situation and feelings during the process of a disagreeable offense. That's not to say that we don't have it in us to have an argument, this is just the best way for us to come out on the other end of an exchange unscathed. We have both matured because of our past relationships and no longer want to live that type of lifestyle.

It feels amazing to be in love with someone who loves you back in the same manner. Knowing that you have someone you can depend on without a doubt creeping in the back of your mind is noteworthy. This man made me view love and the structure of a relationship in a whole other way that I had never wrapped my head around before we met. Sure, I had an idea of what I wanted out of a relationship but never fathomed that I would get everything I wanted to be packed into one finely distinguished man. He makes all others before him seem like a distant memory that happened a lifetime ago. Wow, I really just said that.

He has elevated the bar and because of that; I never have to go searching for love ever in life. I told him when we first met that this was it for me and we were going to stay together no matter what happened from that point on. We are just going to resolve it and make it work. That statement has walked me into many scenarios that have played out in his mind, and although they don't always come out like he thinks they may, we will forever be attached. Which is another thing that keeps us going strong, we have many moments filled with laughter. I can honestly say that there has not been one day that has gone by that I haven't laughed with him or laughed at something that he has done. I will never stop loving this man because his soul is too pure, his emotions are as raw as they come, and he's genuine through and through.

LOOKING BACK

LOOKING BACK, WE made sure to start our relationship by eliminating anything/one who would taint our efforts of becoming a successful couple. The first thing we both did was agree not to have any communication whatsoever with our exes. This made it easy for us to invest all our time and energy into our new beginning without any drama interfering with our start. When one of our exes would try to contact either of us, we wouldn't answer the call/text unless the other was present and we dealt with the situation together. At times, we would even go as far as to take over the conversation when an ex wasn't quite grasping the concept of moving on. Because we had no negative outside influences on what our relationship should be, it was easy for us to mold it into everything that we wanted to get out of it.

There isn't much that I would change about the way we started because we still implement some of those guidelines to this present day. It is very important for us to get away and have our alone time separate from our family time with the children. We continue to dress up and go out on dinner dates, we also find time to get away for at least one weekend a month, and we spoil ourselves with one of our favorite pastimes, which is shopping. He has always and maintains his practice of opening every door for me, walking on the outside of the sidewalk, and holding my hand everywhere we go. Chivalry is *not* dead, it's just not executed as much as it should be today.

Now that we have gotten past getting to know one another and finding a formula that works for us, I can truly say that we mesh well together. I have found that having the same maturity level as my mate is also a plus because we know what we want out of life and we are ready to pursue our goals now that we have found our better halves. It's easy for someone to work for a common goal when you know that both of you are in it for the long haul. Not to take away from anything that we learned from our past relationships, but now we know how to better communicate, love unconditionally, and be rational when it comes to the other person's perceptions.

This is the first relationship that I have ever taken my time with getting to know and understand what *he* needs, how *he* feels, what *he* wants, and what it's going to take for me to meet that for him. In my past, it was more so of someone telling me these things about themselves but not necessarily living a life that mirrored these wants and needs. For example, someone would tell me that they have always wanted to be a power couple but would never go to work and make the same effort as I did to complete that want/need. This time around I did more observing than I did having conversations and figured out what it was that made him long for these things. He has never been the type to shy away from speaking his mind and that's another thing I love and respect him for because sharing your life with someone who is brutally honest is the only way that I can live without being blindsided. I'm glad that I didn't rush this relationship because we got the opportunity to experience one another's needs instead of being told this, that, or the other.

Having a beautiful successful relationship with this man has changed my life for the better. I'm at peace with my past, I have moved forward from negative events that may have damaged me, and I see a better outcome in life because I have someone who is faithful, trustworthy, and stable. I couldn't ask for anything more at this point in my life because it's time to open a new chapter and continue ameliorating my happy ever after without looking back. I believe it's safe to say that I am overly ecstatic about sharing my life with an individual who loves me for every bit of who I am.

We are now working toward the success of our empty nesting if you will. We are solidifying everything that we possibly can to have a promising, impressive, and tranquil retirement. Our goal is to work as hard as possible at this present time, so we can build a life for our future selves. We have many chapters to uncover and additional goals to accomplish. We have both been parents for most of our lives and now that we have found a love worth living for, it will soon be time for us to adventure into a unique situation. I am very happy to say that we are looking forward to a life of our own without the responsibility of children. Most people find one another, fall in love, live together for a while and then have children. We were a bit backwards on that scenario because we came into the relationship already having children, so we don't quite know what it's like for us to just live amongst ourselves in this beautiful bliss of happiness.

MOVING FORWARD

Before him, I gave up all hope of finding a partner/love and once I stopped looking, he came. There are many of you out there who are currently in a relationship with someone that you want to be "the one" and the only way that this is going to happen is if it is truly meant to be. It seems like it took me forever to find the love of my life because of all the failed relationships I had in the past and because of my mindset when it came to the love I wanted and the type of facade that I was receiving. I truly believe that there is someone out there for everyone who is willing to not give up on love. You will find that someone for you whether it's early in life or later in your years. It just takes time to develop the know-how of dealing with someone's baggage, the patients to understand if this person is right for you, and the ability to walk away when you know in your heart of hearts that this is a toxic or tragic relationship. The experience that I am having at this current moment is encouraging to say the least.

As we individually grow into more life experienced, responsible, and enlightened adults, we also accumulate the ability to no longer tolerate abuse, cheating, and dishonesty in our relationships. You should always take note of an individual's actions and less of what comes out of their mouth because words tend to blind us from what is happening right in front of our faces. Just because someone says they love you after you've caught them cheating, doesn't necessarily mean that they love you.

Everything that this man said he was going to do, he has done or is in the process of accomplishing. Things that he said he would change, happened. The things he was honest about, I respected. The same goes for me with him, I gave when he gave and that made it easy for us to gain trust and be able to lean on one another through good and bad endeavors. You can have the same thing as long as you recognize early enough in your relationship that this is what you want. Never try to force love because you will lose that battle every single time. Don't ever try to be something you're not for someone else because they are not falling in love with you, they're falling for the fantasy version of what they believe is an ideal mate.

One thing that I can take away from my present relationship is that he is genuine in every action which in turn complements our relationship. Because we are on the same page, we're growing individually and together. When one person is taking off running and the other person is just testing the waters so to speak, the song never sounds the same. Take the time that your relationship needs to nourish it, make time for one another, and work through the things you thought you'd never get over because your mate makes you feel comfortable enough to share those experiences and you deem them valuable enough to make the change.

Word from the Author

Transformation. When we're young, we allow our friends to take the initiative when applying a nickname to ourselves. As we mature into adults/adulthood it is only right for us to leave those nicknames behind. Sometimes we have to also leave the behavior of those nicknames in the past. We ultimately reinvent ourselves into the person we want others to see. I don't want to perceive myself as someone who is immature when I have clearly matured into someone who was more deserving of a fitting name for myself. When we shred our self of the nickname someone else gave us as a child or young adult, it is then that we realize we have come into a different phase of our life that is more deserving and ready for the transformation of responsibility, adulthood, and acceptance. You are no longer that pipsqueak little kid everyone viewed as the party person, you're to be taken seriously as an adult, business person, educator, or professional in your craft. Why wait to be told to change? You'll eventually get there in realizing that partying, being the class clown, and the butt of the joke is no longer your position. You must now leave that for those coming behind you to experience and learn from. Now as an adult, it's your turn to lead, it's your turn to reassure that those after you don't make the same mistakes you did at their age. Save them the heartache by leading by example because you have been there and done that and you know better at this point in your life.

Damaged goods. Those who let life's stressors consume them, ultimately lose themselves and will never build healthy relationships thereafter. You will climatically diminish yourself as a person, parent, friend, relative, and mate. You become damaged goods and everyone else that you encounter after that point will eventually see that there is no saving you because you don't want to be saved. You run out of excuses when these people try to assist, give advice, or help you in any way, shape, or form. Because of your rejection of their support they write you off as a lost cause and someone who is not worth investing the effort. You will eventually see many people walk out of your life because you refuse to either let it go or stop living in and making others pay for the mistakes of your past. You never want to be seen as someone who is needy, because then you are now someone who needs to be worked on and a relationship should not be a job, it should be a stress relief because you have a partner in life, not a dependent. Although it is difficult to walk away from those we care about, these types of people make it easy for us to eliminate them from our daily routines with the intent to shed the unnecessary drama that they create. Therefore, leaving us with the choice to terminate the relationships of toxic people while we move forward.

Lonely. Never be afraid to be alone because in the end, loving yourself is the most important thing in the world. Knowing your self-worth and projecting that off into the world lets others know how to approach you as a person, how to treat you when sharing your life, and shapes loyalty. I say this because of you, with a set of standards of how people should treat you when in your circle (if they want to stay there), they will respect your wishes, your knowledge, and your space. After a breakup, give yourself time to focus on what went wrong in the relationship so you don't repeat the same mistakes in the future. Use this time to build yourself up, so when the next person comes along, you're not presenting yourself as damaged goods. When you work on yourself spiritually, professionally, and individually, you ultimately attract these features in future mates. They want to be held to the type of standard that you possess (or they will come already packaged up), either way, they will see you as an evenly matched partner.

Some of you may think that I've been through many relationships and how could I give advice? Easy answer, one's failure can ultimately turn into success because they learn to grow from their past mistakes. These failed relationships taught me how to put my needs first because I'm important and you should also note that about yourself. I stand up for myself because no one else will if I don't. I set a certain standard, so I don't repeat my mistakes and I always move forward because my time is valuable and shouldn't be wasted but shared. In the end, I finally got the relationship I wanted from the start, but because I went through cheaters, mental and physical abusers, jealousy, pain, hopelessness, and addictions, I can clearly see that he is my equivalent. I am now able to appreciate the man I have in my life because I know what my past provided and I'm grateful he isn't any of those things. It's also all about being mature enough to handle what you want. Some people say they want a certain type of man or woman and when they get him or her, they say they weren't really my type because they were too this or that.

For example, I thought after all the fighting that I wanted a nice guy, but I didn't because the relationship lacked excitement, adventure, impetuosity, and intensity. I didn't want someone who would yes me to death. I wanted someone who would have his own opinion and tell me no when he didn't agree or thought it would be a great idea to sign off on a crazy notion I came up with at the time. The whole point is for the other person to be right for the relationship, and you must be right for the other person's perception of what they want their relationship to be also.

I survived it all. If I can go through everything that I did and still manage to be a positive person, in the end, you can too as long as you find the willpower to fight through your trials and tribulations. Sure, suffering from pain took away my innocence and the way that I view the world, yet I still hold a certain type of virtuousness because of my ability to remain sheltered.

Eight Rules of Thumb

I have certain rules that I follow that keep me sane/safe when dealing with relationships.

- Get tested so you don't bring health issues to your new partner. This helps you narrow down and treat anything you may have contracted from someone else.
- Always take time to yourself after a breakup. This gives you time to find yourself, so you don't bring unnecessary baggage into a new relationship.
- Don't enter a new relationship when you aren't over the negative aspects of your old relationship. Take a moment to heal. This allows you time to get over old unresolved issues, so you don't make future partners pay for those wrongs.
- Never jump into a relationship because you're lonely, you tend to miss/or dismiss red flags! Don't give an individual an opportunity to slip into your life at a vulnerable point because there are those out there who wait for that moment.
- Take your time getting to know someone before you run off to get married. People show their true colors over time and it's better to find out who they are before you take your vows with this person.

- I generally give a relationship two years to figure out if it'll work. You get to know the person the first year, and they have the second year to work on and fix any issues that are deal breakers for you. After that, it's not worth your time because someone else out there wants to genuinely make the effort to be the person you want to share your life with. I hate that I have given many of my good years to people who could care less.
- Don't waste your time fighting for someone who clearly shows in their actions that they don't value your wants or needs.
- Don't invest in someone who…
  -doesn't save you money because they aren't concerned with being stable.
  -lives recklessly because your well-being will never be as important as theirs
  -doesn't have a sense of humor because your happiness is something they can live without.

imstillaworkinprogress.com
#walkaway
#workinprogress

About the Author

Alexandra Lee Paige is a life and empowerment coach, CEO and founder of a life coaching company where she provides guidance to those seeking positive outcomes for their relationship issues. She has an Associate of Arts with a concentration in Psychology, a Bachelor of Science in Psychology, and is currently obtaining a Masters in Marriage and Family Therapy. Her story is triumphant and is the reason why she dedicates herself to the field of personal and life improvement.

Mrs. Paige is family oriented and a go-getter, which shows in her determination to enrichen relationships between couples and solidify family bonds with others. She has two sons herself and understands how important it is to have a support system when traveling through life. Family is always first on her list, even though she has been through trials and tribulations, she learns from her mistakes and implements those lessons in her life moving forward.

Mrs. Paige remains positive even though others have entered her world who possessed ill-willed intentions, malice behavioral traits, and venom field hearts. She has managed to overcome physical/mental abuse, sexual assaults, and a life-changing occurrence. Still, she stands unbroken and ready for war!

Alexandra's gladiator approach to life is addicting, contagious, and unquestionably as genuine as one may assume.

www.ingramcontent.com/pod-product-compliance
Lightning Source LLC
Chambersburg PA
CBHW020807160426
43192CB00006B/476